Money Enough for LIFE?

A Financial Roadmap for All Ages

Money Enough for LIFE?

A Financial Roadmap for All Ages

By C. Pete Benson
and Jon S. Maxson

Copyright ©2014 by C. Pete Benson and Jon S. Maxson

All rights reserved. No part of this book may be used or reproduced in any manner whatsoever, without express written permission, except for brief quotations for use in reviews or critical articles.

Table of Contents

PREFACE

From a financial point of view, retirement is like getting re-born. One day you are swaddled in the comfort of your job, receiving your regular paycheck, and the next day that umbilical connection is severed and you are on your own. From now on you will be writing your own paycheck. You will also begin to view your resources differently, now that you realize just how non-renewable most of them are.

Remember all those years you put money aside from your paycheck into your retirement account? Well, now those resources have to carry you through, but for how long? The rest of your life! And just how long do you think that will be? Most of us are aware that we will, as Shakespeare put it, "shuffle off this mortal coil," but most also hope that won't happen any time soon. Let's face it, most people, want the sand in the hourglass to stay in the top part as long as possible. But will we have enough money to last? That question is on the minds of many retirees and soon-to-be retirees these days. And it's not about the money; not really. It's about independence. We want to be self-sustaining as long as we live without being a burden to our loved ones. In fact, we would like to have enough resources to leave a legacy for those we love.

The Allianz Life Insurance Company of North America conducted a survey in May 2010 that sampled income perceptions of more than 3,200 baby boomers (born between 1946 and 1964) ranging in age from 44 to 75. Guess what they discovered was the number one fear among most of them when it came to growing older. Death? No. Snakes and spiders? Inflation or health care costs? Not even close. Their number one fear was outliving their money.

Longevity – Blessing or Curse?

If you travel to the Middle Eastern country of Jordan, one of the historic sites on the Lands of the Bible tour is Mount Nebo. As mountains go, it's not that high – a little over 3,000 feet. But according to the Bible, Mount Nebo is where Moses stood and gazed over into the Promised Land he would never enter. Sure enough, on a clear day you can make out such landmarks as the Dead Sea, the Jordan River, Bethlehem and Jerusalem. Moses, who is considered a prophet by Muslims, Christians, and Jews alike, was 120 years old when he died. He left behind a prayer that surfaces years later in the Bible book of Psalms about the human lifespan. Here is an excerpt:

"The length of our days is seventy years—or eighty if we have the strength…." Psalms 90:10

Other Modern English versions also do the math for you. The New World Translation says: "The span of our life is 70 years, or 80 if one is especially strong…" Moses must have been "especially strong" to have lived so long.

So there's good news and bad news. Which do you want first? The good news? Okay, the good news is people of your generation are living longer. As a class, baby boomers are living longer than their parents lived. Whether it is because of better medicine, a decline in tobacco use, or genetics, we don't know. But on average boomers are outliving their parents' generation by almost a decade. At the turn of the century, in 1900, the average life expectancy in the United States was 47, In 1960 it was 69, in 2004, 80. And in 2012, it was 86. Keep in mind, too, that we are dealing with averages. The way life expectancy tables work is quite complicated. The formula says, in essence, that if you live to be 50, your odds of making it to 70 just went up. If you make it to 70, your chances of reaching 90 increase exponentially.

Centenarians used to be a rarity, but more and more people aren't just living to 100, they're even making it past 105. How many of them are there? According to the 2010 census there were 53,364 Americans age 100 or older; the 1950 census recorded only 2,300 centenarians. It is projected that in the future, millions will live past the age of 100. Pete and Ginnie Benson are acquainted with a man by the name of "Smiles" Green who lives on the small island of Grand Manan, where they both grew up. In 2013, he celebrated his 100th birthday, lives alone, drives a car, and still hunts.

For the first time in history there are now more seniors than there are teenagers. If you are a baby boomer, it is probable your parents either died during their working years or shortly afterward. Many of your generation will live 20 to 30 years after retirement. The number of seniors aged 65 and older in the United States is expected to more than double from 39 million today to 89 million in 2050. Some seniors will be retired for more years than they spent in the workforce. Even today we have clients who find themselves in this situation.

So, what's the bad news? The bad news is that we are living longer. Wait a minute; I thought that was the good news! What could possibly be negative about living a longer life? One of the major issues is it takes money to live. If you haven't taken steps to plan properly, you may run out. You could lose your independence and become a burden on others or a ward of the state. Just the thought of that makes most people shudder.

Other Retirement Challenges

The three-legged stool of retirement used to be (a) pension (b) savings, and (c) Social Security. If you just said, "What pension?" you are not alone. Pensions are going the way of drive-in theaters, cheap gasoline and rotary dial phones. If you have a pension, consider yourself one of the fortunate few. Private corporations have all but eliminated defined benefit pension plans these days. Most retirees today will look to their 401(k)'s and Social Security as the wellsprings from which they will write their own paycheck in retirement. But many are unaware of the fact that the 401(k) and accompanying mutual funds that got them *to* retirement are not the right vehicles to get them *through* retirement.

Three Legged
Stool of Retirement

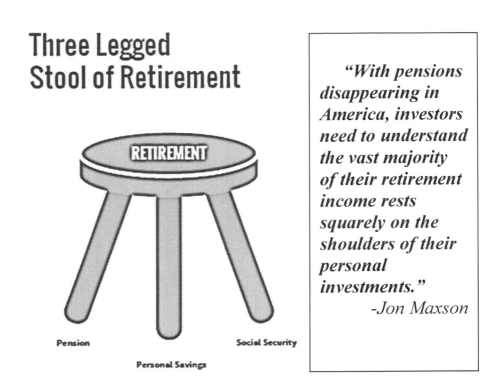

"With pensions disappearing in America, investors need to understand the vast majority of their retirement income rests squarely on the shoulders of their personal investments."
-Jon Maxson

Shortly after the 2008 stock market crash, a couple came to our office asking for help. They had attended a seminar we conducted on retirement income planning. These people were intelligent and well-educated. He was a professor and she was manager and part owner of a boutique flower shop.

The couple brought a shoe box with them which contained the latest statements from their retirement accounts. He passed the box across the desk with a sigh.

"Read them and weep," he said. "That's what we have been doing for the last two weeks."

The pair had saved diligently, contributing the maximum to their retirement accounts, all of which were invested in mutual funds, and all of which had lost value – more than 38% - during the Wall Street tumble. They planned on retiring when he turned 65; she would sell her share of the florist shop and they would finally achieve their life-long "blue highway" dream. They always wanted to take their camper along the back roads of America – the highways that always show up blue on the road maps – and take their time seeing the country. A history professor, he was interested in reading every historical marker they encountered. An amateur photographer, she wanted to document their trip with her new digital camera. Those plans would have to wait, however. The way they figured it, they would have to work at least another three years and pare down their lifestyle, in order to retire. They would just wait and see if the "blue highway" dream tour was even a possibility at that time.

It would have done little good to tell them their most critical mistake was not being as involved in their financial affairs as they should have been. They were probably painfully aware of it at that point. While they had saved up almost a half million dollars for their retirement, they left the details to others, unaware of the risk they were taking with the investments. They were much too busy with their careers to worry about what was on the statements they received. They confessed that sometimes they would let months go by before they would even open them. They were, after all, being looked after by professionals, weren't they?

This couple is not unique. In fact, they are rather typical as the aforementioned survey reveals. In this book we will tackle the subject of stock market risk and how to gauge how much is too much.

We will also look at Social Security. According to the Social Security Administration, in 2013 almost 58 million Americans received $816 billion in Social Security benefits. When the program was introduced in 1935, it was meant to merely be a supplement for retirees, not a full pension. Yet currently, Social Security represents 39% of the income for most of the elderly in America and 23% of married couples. In addition, approximately 46% of unmarried persons rely on Social Security for 90% or more of their income. We have found that most retirees don't understand just how many options come with Social Security and what impact those decisions may have on their financial lives.

Through the pages of this book, our aim is to bridge the "awareness gap." Statistically, baby boomers are the largest generation in the history of America, numbering around 77 million. They started turning 65 in 2011; that means approximately 10,000 boomers are retiring every single day. When we first came across that statistic it occurred to us that in one week's time, the number of Americans lining up for Medicare, signing up for Social Security, and entering retirement would fill up nearby LP field in Nashville, where the Tennessee Titans of the National Football League play their home games. That mental picture is startling. And what is an even more sobering thought is that, according to the Allianz survey, the majority of them are unprepared for what lies ahead. When the pollsters asked how much annual income they would need when they retired, most retirees indicated that a median income of $59,000 per year ought to do it. But when the same folks were asked the follow-up question of how much they would have to save to create that amount, their guesses were way low. The number most came up with was only a third of what was actually needed.

That research underscores the conclusion that we, the founders of Beacon Capital Management, came to in our unofficial poll, which is that, while most baby boomers are great consumers and excellent spenders, they have, as a class, proven to be ineffective savers and poor planners. We felt if there was ever a time when we need to live up to our firm's name and let our collective light shine like a penetrating beacon in the fog of outdated and unworkable ideas, it is now. You will see as you continue reading that the pages of this book contain much of the conservative investing philosophy and lifetime income generating strategies that we have developed over the last decade or so – ideas thousands of retirees now subscribe to. In so doing, we have attempted to put together purpose-driven retirement roadmaps for all our clients.

In other words, *Money Enough for LIFE?*

SECTION 1

BEGINNING YOUR LIFE WITH MONEY
(Ages 20-40)

CHAPTER ONE

Everyone Needs a Plan

*"If you live like no one else, then you can live
and give like no one else."* - Dave Ramsey

Who knows if it really happened or not, but the story is told that
Albert Einstein, the famous physicist, was once traveling on a train
when the conductor came down the aisle, punching the tickets of every
passenger. When he came to Einstein, the bushy-haired scientist
fumbled around in his vest pockets. He couldn't find his ticket, so he
searched his trouser pockets. It wasn't there, so he looked in his
briefcase but couldn't find it. Finally, he looked in the seat beside him;
he still couldn't find it.

The conductor said, "Dr. Einstein, I know who you are; we all
know who you are. I'm sure you bought a ticket. Don't worry about it."

Einstein nodded appreciatively. The conductor continued down the
aisle punching tickets. As he was ready to move to the next car, he
turned around and saw the famous man down on his hands and knees,
looking under his seat for his ticket.

The conductor rushed back and said, "Dr. Einstein, Dr. Einstein,
don't worry, I know who you are. No problem. You don't need a ticket.
I'm sure you bought one."

Einstein looked at him and said, "Young man, I too, know who I
am. What I don't know is where I'm going."

The point of the story is that traveling without a destination is
pointless. Several quotes exist in the archives of literature about this.
Author Lewis Carroll (*Alice in Wonderland*) is quoted as saying: "If
you don't know where you are going, any road will get you there."

Actually, the quote is a paraphrased rendering of a conversation between Alice and the Cheshire Cat in chapter six of Carroll's famous book:

> *"Would you tell me, please, which way I ought to go from here?"*
> *"That depends a good deal on where you want to get to," said the Cat.*
> *"I don't much care where--" said Alice.*
> *"Then it doesn't matter which way you go," said the Cat.*

The most colorful quote, however, is attributed to Yogi Berra, the master of the unintentional (maybe) malapropism. There are actually two versions of this quote:

"If you don't know where you are going, you might wind up someplace else," and "You've got to be very careful if you don't know where you are going, because you might not get there." Whether the famous Yankee catcher ever actually uttered either one or not, it still makes the point splendidly that to get anywhere you must have a destination in mind.

As financial advisors, such a concept is a core belief for us. You never plan to fail…you just fail to plan. We are big believers that successful people – in every area of life but especially financially – are planners.

It's even biblical to plan.

"A prudent man foresees the difficulties ahead and prepares (_PLANS_) for them; the simpleton goes blindly on and suffers the consequences." Proverbs 22:3

"But don't begin until you count the cost. For who would begin construction of a building without first calculating the cost to see if there is enough money to finish it?" Luke 14:28 - *The Living Bible.*

The following story told by Pete Benson illustrates the importance of planning:

A few years ago my wife Ginnie and I were invited to hold a financial conference in Velden, Austria, for a group of missionaries who had come together from their assignments all over Europe. It was a long trip from central Tennessee to Austria and back, so Ginnie and I decided to make a two-week vacation out of it.

For several months, in our spare time, we got on the internet to search out various places we wanted to visit on the trip. It was daunting trying to figure out which cities and what countries we wanted to see. We also tried to iron out which hotels we would stay in, but there were thousands to pick from. Then, there were the little niggling details about transportation. What was the best way to get from place to place? We had no idea. There was conflicting advice on the internet and it was difficult to find unbiased information. The big pieces of the puzzle were clear to us. We wanted to spend a day or two in Paris, visit Germany, and see Venice and Rome. What we couldn't put together were the details of how to do that in the most efficient manner.

We worked on it a few months ourselves, but as the time for the trip approached we were feeling less and less confident. We decided to swallow our pride and hire a professional to map it all out for us. We had no idea what a satisfying experience this would be.

When the travel agent met with us, we knew we had made the right decision. She asked us dozens of questions to get a feel for what we really wanted out of the trip, then mapped out a wonderful itinerary for us. She left nothing to chance. All the details were neatly buttoned up. On the last visit to the travel agent's office she presented us with a thick book consisting of every detail of the trip from beginning to end. We knew the times of every flight, and how to get to each hotel, train station, restaurant, and village along the way. Our delightful 13-day European vacation took us through four countries without a single hitch. We were so thankful that we didn't try "winging it" the way we started. Who knows where we would have ended up had it not been for the able assistance of a fully-trained, competent professional travel planner?

How unfortunate it is that people will spend as many as 80,000 hours working for more than 40 years, and yet not spend the time necessary to map out their finances and plan for their retirement. From our vantage point as financial counselors, far too many people seem to be ambling aimlessly along, hoping and praying that everything will just turn out all right. Hope is not a plan.

All through our lives we need to be following a plan of some kind. In our earlier years, we need to follow a budget. We must set aside an emergency fund, plan for children's education, plan how and when we are going to buy our next car, decide when and whether we are going to purchase or rent a home, etc.

Before the days of the GPS (Global Positioning System) we had the good, old-fashioned road map. It was unthinkable for a family to go off on a long vacation involving automobile travel to unfamiliar places, without first obtaining a map on which to mark out the route. As a matter of fact, at every gas station there was a rack of complimentary maps, they were free with a fill-up. Sadly, the vast majority of Americans spend more time planning their next vacation than they do planning the rest of their lives in retirement.

Determine Values and Set Goals

Planning starts with making some simple (often not easy, but simple) decisions and putting them down in writing.

VALUES - What are the most important things in life to you? Have you ever listed them? This is a crucial step in planning. It's like plotting your destination before a trip. These values may change over time. For example, when you are young, just starting out in life, your values may center on entertainment, obtaining nice cars, and a big home. Later, it may be providing an education for your children or becoming debt-free. Still later on in life, your values may lean more in the direction of providing an income for retirement, traveling, giving money to your church or other charities, or perhaps arranging your affairs so you are able to retire early. Whatever the case, name your top five values in order of priority and *write them down.* Why is it important to put them in writing? One reason is that the very exercise of writing them down forces you to organize them. Also, putting your values in writing sets you up nicely for the second step.

GOALS - Set your goals. If values are the destination, then goals represent the roadmap that will take you there.

Charles Schulz, creator of the cartoon strip *Peanuts*, was capable of conveying many thought-provoking ideas through the little round-headed children he drew. Take, for example, the one where the strip's protagonist, Charlie Brown, appears in the first frame pulling back the string of a bow. The arrow is pointed slightly up. We can't see the target but we assume he is shooting at something.

In the second frame we see Charlie Brown over by a fence where his arrow has embedded itself in the wood.

In the third frame, Charlie is painting a bull's eye around the arrow.

Then Lucy comes running up in the last frame and says, "Charlie Brown, you blockhead! That's not how you do it!" To which Charlie Brown responds: "But this way, Lucy, I never miss."

Do you know anyone who operates that way regarding their finances? Hoping for success with no goal in mind? Charlie Brown made no apologies for taking such a shortcut, did he? In fact, he rationalized that if he had no target he couldn't miss! When it comes to financial matters, that is unfortunately how many people go through life.

The "Tyranny of the Urgent"

In the 1960s, Charles Hummel published a little booklet called *Tyranny of the Urgent*, which quickly became a best seller and a business classic. In it, Hummel pointed out that there is a regular tension between things that are ***urgent*** and things that are ***important.*** Far too often, says Hummel, the urgent wins.

In the business world the urgent demands of your boss, your client, or petty office relationships, can often take priority over important things like thoroughly completing a task before starting the next one, or building unity in a work team that would instill camaraderie and longevity. The *urgent*, though less important, gets priority, while the *important* is put on the back burner. That's why it is tyrannical. While you are yielding to that impulse, greasing the squeaky wheel, you are delayed from your destination.

In Charlie Brown's case, he didn't aim and then shoot; he shot and then aimed. How convenient it is to just draw a target where your arrow lands! Charlie Brown, like many people, wanted instant gratification with no effort. What is our "tyranny of the urgent"? And how do we know we are hitting the target (goal) if there is no target (we have not set a goal)?

When it comes to financial planning, an "accountability partner" can help you keep on track with accomplishing your goals. You cannot work your plan if you don't have one. Once you have one, it won't work unless you work it. Put succinctly, "plan your work… and work your plan."

CHAPTER TWO

Why Your Budget Rules

"A budget is people telling their money where to go instead of wondering where it went" - John Maxwell

Much has been written and said about King Solomon. The Bible tells us that in addition to being the world's **richest** man, he was also the world's **wisest** man. God appeared to Solomon in a dream and promised him anything he asked. Solomon chose understanding and discernment. According to the scriptures, God was so pleased with the request that he granted it, along with great riches and power.

The third king of Israel proved to be a prolific writer, poet, and scientist. His skills in architecture and management turned Israel into the showplace of the Middle East. He is credited with writing much of the book of Proverbs, the Song of Solomon, the book of Ecclesiastes, and two psalms.

Proverbs 27:23 says, "Be sure to know the condition of your flocks, give careful attention to your herds." In those days, flocks and herds were how one's wealth was measured. In today's world, that would mean: "Know the condition of your financial household." Herds and flocks were exposed to the elements. They were sometimes targets of wild animals like lions and bears. Winters in Jerusalem could be quite cold; summers quite dry. If you had owned animals in ancient Palestine, and you wished to preserve your wealth, you would have paid attention to where your herds and flocks were grazing. Depending on how wealthy you were, you would have even paid shepherds to watch after the physical needs of the animals. You would have known "what time it was", so to speak, as it related to caring for the animals and providing the right conditions for offspring.

So how about you? Do you know the condition of your financial household? Do you know where you stand? Do you have a written budget that your family tries to follow? If not, what guides your daily and weekly spending decisions? According to the Wall Street Journal, nearly 70% of Americans live paycheck to paycheck. This simple truth comes to mind: "If your **outgo** exceeds your **income**, then your **upkeep** will be your **downfall.**"

Having a budget in place is, in effect, having a "spending plan." Our observation is that most people resist having a budget because they see it as too restrictive. Yes, a budget is a restraint, but, then again, so are the guard rails on curvy mountain roads.

Budgets Keep Us Out of Trouble

The most dangerous road in the world is Bolivia's "Death Road" in South America. It is also called the "Road of Fate." If it sounds ominous, it's because it is! A BBC documentary claimed that 200-300 travelers on the narrow mountain road are killed every year, most of them plunging off cliffs that are over 1,000 feet high. On most sections the road is only one lane wide and there are no guard rails!

Not having a budget and then spending recklessly is like tearing down the "Road of Fate" without guardrails. It could send you financially over the edge in a hurry. We Americans adore our freedoms and we despise being confined or restrained. But, like those guardrails that we enjoy on our good, old American roads, the budget is our friend.

A budget is nothing more than a short-range plan for how to spend money during the next twelve months. Instead of restricting your freedom, a well-structured budget should expand your quality of life by helping you live within your means. A written budget (spending plan) guides you, just like those yellow and white lines on a highway, helping you decide how to spend your money.

One woman, discussing her inability to save money, said, "I just don't know where my money goes." That's understandable. How can you know where it goes unless you track it? We often recommend that people track every single purchase and expenditure of household money for at least 90 days. Sure, it may be a tedious process, but it teaches a great deal. One couple with whom we counseled, agreed to do this. They each carried with them a small black book. Every time a purchase was made, regardless of how insignificant, it went into the "little black book." At the end of each week, the pair would reconcile their books by adding up and categorizing the purchases. If children are involved who have spending privileges, we suggest you get them in on the process. Make it a family meeting at the end of each week. Tally up the expenditures monthly, consolidate the balances, and begin again.

What's that? You say that is just a little low tech for you? Understandable. We do, after all, live in the age of computers and electronic spreadsheets. All you have to do is enter the phrase "budget apps" in your search bar and you will come up with applications for every operating system out there. If you have a smartphone, you will be able to compile your entries into a spreadsheet and sort according to the categories provided in the program.

The point is, regardless of how you do it, put the guardrails up, especially if you are on dangerous ground, and protect your financial center. Here are five pointed reasons why we recommend a budget:

Keeps you focused on your goals – The discipline of a budget will allow you to eliminate wasteful spending so you can save *within the guardrails* for what you want. Think about it. You can either have what money will buy or you can have the money, but you can't have both. Once you've spent it, it's gone. The budget forces you to map out your goals. Want to go on a Caribbean cruise? Write it into the budget and go for it.

Prevents you from spending money you don't have – Just ask anyone who has fallen into the quicksand of high-dollar credit card debt; there are plenty of them around. According to 2012 statistics released by the United States Federal Reserve System, the total U.S. credit card debt was $793.1 billion which would place the average credit card debt per household at $15,799 and rising. To show how large a number that really is, CNN took an interesting angle on this story and looked at countries with a gross domestic product (GDP) of less than $500 billion. It noted that Poland, Belgium, Sweden, Saudi Arabia and Taiwan all had GDPs that were less than this.

What did we do before we had plastic? We lived within our means. But now that we can buy now and pay later, it is tempting to abuse the privilege. If you establish a budget and stick with it you will never get caught in that trap.

Enables you to retire with peace of mind – Let's face it, before you can retire with security, you must save. You can't save if you live paycheck to paycheck or if you live beyond your means. Those dots are easy enough to connect. But beyond that is building investment contributions into your budget. If you are young, your older self will someday thank your younger self if you save money instead of spend it.

Helps you handle emergencies – Life is full of surprises. You could get hurt, sick, or experience a death in the family. You could lose your job or go through a divorce. The transmission could fall out of your car. If you are strapped for cash, you will have to go into debt, and we have already established that you don't want any part of consumer credit card debt. Your budget should include an emergency fund. How much should it contain? Well, that's up to you, but we recommend six months income. The emergency fund should be as liquid as possible.

Holds up a mirror to your spending habits - You may not think twice about buying a $4. cup of coffee, but your budget will. It will make you look closely at how you spend money and it will make you look for ways to conserve. Do you really need a 600-channel cable TV agreement, how many do you really watch, anyway? For that matter, do you even need cable TV if you have credit card debt you need to pay off?

Better mental health – Have you ever lost sleep over money? Have you ever worried about how you were going to pay the bills? A budget allows you to get back possession of your own financial ship and take control again. Once you do that, you can sleep better at night and won't be nearly as irritable.

We could go on and on, but you get the idea. Some refer to a budget as the "B" word. So do we: ***Blessing!***

CHAPTER THREE

It's All about Choices

*"You should have two financial goals in life: to make a little money **first**, and then to make a little money **last**." -* Unknown

Darren Hardy, in his book, *The Compound Effect,* has this to say about choices: "We all come into this world the same: naked, scared, and ignorant. After the grand entrance, the life we end up with is simply an accumulation of all the <u>choices</u> we make. Our choices can be our best friend or our worst enemy. They can deliver us to our goals or send us orbiting into a galaxy far, far away."

That sentiment certainly applies to financial success (or failure, as the case may be). We all have opportunity. We all make daily choices about money. The financial life we end up with is simply an accumulation of all the choices we make. Consider that every one dollar bill we bring into our lives through our work can only be spent one time. We are faced with so many choices of what to do with that one dollar. But again, once it's gone, it's gone forever. You may get *another* dollar at some point, but the one you spent is gone.

Perhaps as a youngster you went to the county fair, or some other amusement park. Let's say your parents gave you $10 (maybe with inflation that should be $30 now) and said you could spend it on anything you wished, but that was all you were going to get. So many choices! You walk the midway making value judgments. Sure, you would like to try the ring toss for a dollar, but that would be 10% of your fair allowance down the tubes and you probably wouldn't win one of those stuffed animals anyway. So, you pass the ring toss by. You can't experience all the rides for $10, so you choose carefully, based on how thrilling the ride looks to you and how much it costs. Perhaps you save one last dollar for cotton candy or some other exotic fair food.

Any of that ring a bell? Even if you never went to a fair as a youth, you can still identify with the principle. You have several choices available to you, but you may only choose one. As soon as you receive a sum of money, you are faced with many choices. You can spend it all, spend a portion of it, save a portion of it, or save all of it. If you choose to spend it, you may spend it foolishly or wisely. You may also invest it.

You are not forced to 'spend' it all; you could give some of it away to your favorite charity. Theologian John Wesley had the following credo: *"I want to earn all I can, so I can save all I can, so I can give all I can!"* Not a bad source of motivation. The point is, your choices are manifold.

The Evils of Credit Card Debt

"How in the world did this happen?" asked the shocked couple when they discovered their son, a freshman in college, was suddenly $5,000 in debt to a credit card company.

"They sent the card to me, Mom," replied the son. "What was I supposed to do?"

The couple began receiving calls from a credit card company wanting to know why no payments had been made on *their* account. After a few minutes of protesting that they had no account with this company, it became clear it was their son who had run up the debt. He signed up for the card at a mall "because they were giving away free t-shirts."

It should go without saying that signing up for a credit card when you have no job is an unwise choice. Yet thousands of college students fall victim to this scheme each year. A CNN Money article dated May 17, 2013, states that over 80% percent of college students have at least one credit card, and the average balance is approximately $3,000.

This is troubling on several levels, not least of which is the jeopardy in which students are placing their futures. The idea of buy now and pay later is a siren song some young people find irresistible. Let's face it – kids these days don't need a lesson on how to spend money; that skill seems to come as natural to them as swimming does to a fish. What would be helpful, however, is more education on spending wisely, saving, and building a sound financial future. Our informal poll shows that personal finance is not offered at any of the universities with which we are acquainted, and it does not seem to be included in most high school curriculums. Why is that? Isn't this a very crucial part of becoming a responsible citizen and entering life as a productive and financially stable adult? We believe that preparing our children for the real world should include this type of training. Yet there are no courses on "How to Read a Bank Statement," or Compound Interest 101. Students are generally not taught the principles of saving for retirement, how to invest, or how to avoid the trap of consumer credit card debt…none of it. Sending our young people out into the world without a foundation in financial education is a little like putting them behind the wheel of a car without basic driver's training. As a result of this omission, many young people enter the real world without a clue as to how to manage their money. Is personal finance over the heads of young people? Not at all! You don't even have to be all that good at math. It seems these life lessons, unless taught to them by responsible parents, are left for our youth to discover on their own.

The parents of the college-age son who was $5,000 in credit card debt, commendably held him responsible for the debt by insisting that he work to pay the credit card off. While doing so required that he work two jobs over the summer and abandon his plans for a vacation with his friends, the result was a valuable lesson he will not soon forget.

Birth of the Credit Card

You can probably tell by now that we feel strongly enough about credit card debt to call it "evil." That may sound a little harsh, but not from the perspective of financial planners who have seen this derail the financial lives of so many. The comparison of quick gratification and painful payback to illegal narcotics is not too big of a stretch. We hate to see young people get hooked on easy borrowing because the pay back can be so painful.

A look back in history reveals that store credit has been around for ages. In the old days, farmers would run up a tab at the local general store and pay it off when their crops came in. Large department stores in the cities extended credit to those they deemed "good-paying customers." Most young people today don't know what a "lay away" program is, but large department stores would put, say, an article of clothing aside and allow the customer to come in and pay on the item incrementally until the balance was satisfied, and then take the item home. Credit buying replaced that idea.

Revolving credit appeared during the economic boom that followed World War II. The "Charge-It" card was the first bank credit card, introduced in 1946 by John Biggins, a banker in Brooklyn, New York. It was a local affair at first, with only a few major department stores participating. When you bought something with your "Charge-It" card, the bill went to Biggins' bank where the charges were deducted from your account there. That was the big catch. If you wanted the convenience of buy now, pay later, you had to have an account at Biggins' bank.

In 1950, Diners' Club credit cards were born. In those days, it was a real club for people who wanted to eat now and pay later. Within just a few years the card was in widespread use and could be used to buy merchandise. After Diners' Club came Master Charge (now MasterCard) and Bank Americard (now Visa). Today there are more than 60 million credit card holders in America. The average number of credit cards held is seven and the average balance carried on each card is $2,500.

The Minimum Payment Trap

Many young consumers fall into the "minimum payment due" trap and dig themselves deeper and deeper into the hole. If you want to make the credit card companies love you, just pay them the minimum payment due each month. Why? Because you will likely never pay off the balance, which means you will be paying interest to the credit card company forever. Let's do a little math: The minimum payment is usually between 2%-4% of the total due. So let's say you have a credit card balance of $5,000 and the credit card company is extremely generous to you and gives you a 2% minimum payment. Fantastic! All you have to pay them is $100 and you can forget about it until next month. If you don't charge anything else to the card and you pay your minimum payment on time, your balance would go down by the payment amount, less the interest charges for that month.

So where's the trap?

Here's the trap: The next month, when you get your statement, you will see the minimum payment is a little lower. If you just pay that minimum payment, you are doing two things: (1) prolonging the period of time the company can charge you interest, and (2) tempting yourself to use it again. In this illustration, if your credit card interest rate was 18%, and you paid the minimum payment on an original debt of $5,000, it would take you 472 months to pay the card off *with total interest payments of $13,396!* Our advice, dear young reader, is to pay off the card, and cut it up into little pieces as soon as possible. Failing that, pick an amount you can afford and pay that amount every month, regardless of what the minimum payment is, and **then** get out the scissors and cut it up in little pieces. You will be happy you did. If you are the average American with seven credit cards on which you carry a total balance of more than $15,000 annually, let us suggest that you find which ones charge the most interest and pay those off first. When you pay off the last dollar, have a card-cutting ceremony. There is a reason why you hear expressions such as "in over your head" and "under water" used for describing debt. When you are drowning in debt, you can't breathe. There is no sweeter air than that lungful you gulp when you come out of the water after having held your breath for a minute or so. It's almost as good as the debt-free feeling you get when you pay off your last charge card. The only way to make compound interest work *for* you is to be in a position where it is not working *against* you.

Live Below Your Means

You have probably heard the wise advice, "Always live within your means." We encourage young people to live *below* their means so they can afford to save for the future. Easy to say and hard to do, but buy everything cash. Owe nothing but possibly a mortgage payment. Develop the habit of saving early. Your older self will thank your younger self some-day. The temptation is to rationalize that if something is on sale it's prudent to buy it now when the time is right. If that purchase is with cash, we agree with you if you really *need* that item, either now or in the future. But if you put the purchase on a credit card, you may end up paying 40% more in interest to get that 20% markdown. You have to ask yourself, "Do I really want to pay *interest* on a new pair of designer jeans?"

Take Charge of Your Own Financial Future

Want some sage advice on how to take charge of your financial future? Read books such as this one on personal finance. As stated previously, we believe public education in this area is sadly lacking in America. But, you can educate yourself. Also, don't try to keep up with your peers. Develop a budget and stay within it. Know how much you are spending, saving, and earning. Know where you have your savings and why you have it there. Ask questions of your banker, or whoever represents the custodian where you have placed your "rainy day money." If you get financial statements, open them, read them, and if you don't understand them, ask questions until you do. Here are some more gems:

Pinch pennies; they make dollars later on - Within reason, cut costs whenever possible. Clip coupons. Eat before you go to the movies instead of "investing" in popcorn, candy, and drinks. Come to think about it, wait until the movie comes out on DVD and rent it from the dollar vending machine around the corner! Eat before you go to a restaurant and then order an appetizer. Have fun, but make a supreme effort to stick to your budget and your savings program, without being too weird.

Stay on budget during the holidays - This is a tough one, especially if you are the kind to easily get caught up in the joy of the Christmas season. If you are the gregarious sort, and you love giving gifts, plan well ahead when *Jingle Bells* aren't ring-ting-tingling and you aren't humming carols. That way you will be able to accommodate your holiday spirit without becoming a total Grinch. Perhaps you will have the retirement you are saving for *and* avoid all the lines.

Develop good spending/saving habits - If you want to create a new habit, whether it's eating a piece of fruit for lunch, getting more exercise, or posting your blog every day, behavior experts say it takes 21 days to form a new habit. Once you are in a habit of consulting your budget before spending money frivolously, you will do it automatically, even if you do the math in your head. It's the same with savings. Chunk that money into your savings account every paycheck until it becomes your financial heartbeat. Years from now, somewhere on a sandy beach without a care in the world, your older self will offer a toast to your younger self and sincerely thank you.

Understanding why you're spending money and saving money will help you develop good habits. We heard it said once that people tend to buy things they don't need, with money they don't have, to impress people they really don't like. There is a ring of truth in that.

CHAPTER FOUR

Invest in Yourself and Your Future

"There is nothing wrong with men possessing riches.
The wrong comes when riches possess men."
- Billy Graham

There is an old saying, "You don't go to a poor man to learn the secret of obtaining wealth." In today's modern world, when you utter the name of Warren Buffet, people perk up their ears just like they did in that old E.F. Hutton commercial of the 1980s.? It doesn't take a rocket scientist to figure out why. Forbes magazine puts this lively octogenarian at number four on the richest people in the world list, at $57.1 billion. That's one reason we tend to listen when he speaks. The other reason is because he made all that money by investing. But with all his wealth, Warren Buffet has nothing on King Solomon, the third regent to occupy the throne of the nation of Israel in Bible times.

We met King Solomon and heard a sample of his wisdom in an earlier chapter. Since his name, his poetry, and his life story appear in the Bible, which is the world's number one best seller of all time, you could say that wise King Solomon has received significantly more press than the founder of Berkshire Hathaway.

As far as how rich King Solomon was, if you measured his wealth in terms of today's monetary values, he would be richer than any of the people on the Forbes list. According to the Bible books of 1 Kings and 2 Chronicles, Solomon received 25 tons of gold per year. This did not include his income from trade and other businesses. It also did not include the annual tribute paid to him by other kings and governors. He was reportedly so rich, that during the years of his reign over Jerusalem, his immense wealth caused silver to be considered of little value and as common as rocks. So, if our ears don't perk up when King Solomon speaks, aka the E.F. Hutton commercial, perhaps they should. Here's a sample of what the richest man who ever lived had to say about spending and saving:

"There is treasure to be desired and oil in the dwelling of the wise; but a foolish man spends it all up." **Proverbs 21:20**

Put another way, "If you are smart, you will save for the future. It's really stupid to spend every dime you get."

Americans, it seems, aren't listening to this wisdom however, if statistics about their spending and saving habits are to be believed. Here's a quote from the news channel CNBC that appeared in May, 2013:

"Many economists and fund industry experts say that unless Americans change their spending habits and learn how to save, we will soon be facing a full blown retirement crisis and it may be turn out to be a deeper and more harrowing experience than many have already envisioned."

In May of the previous year, CNBC also reported that about half of 3,000 Americans polled in a recent survey said they were spending more than they earned at least a few months each year, adding that part of the problem may be that "a lot of Americans don't see saving as part of their lifestyle."

"Half of those surveyed do not set monthly savings goals for themselves," the article added. "Of those who are spending more than they earn, 36% are dipping into savings, 22% use a credit card and 8% are borrowing money in other ways."

This was mentioned earlier but bears repeating. One thing that has always concerned us is that American school children don't learn much about personal finance through the school system. Why is that? Ask most high school seniors to explain compound interest or dollar-cost averaging and you would get a blank stare. So it shouldn't surprise us that many Americans can't connect the dots between overspending and financial risk. A 2012 survey by the Consumer Federation of America revealed that only 44% of Americans understand that a credit score measures the risk of not repaying a loan, rather than their debt or financial resources. Another 2012 survey by Rasmussen reported that only half of the 3,000 Americans surveyed said they have a monthly budget, and almost 25% have no liquid assets, meaning savings that can easily be converted into cash. Meanwhile, 10% of families had more than $30,000 in debt as of 2011, up from 8.5 percent of families in 2009, according to the survey.

It wouldn't be an understatement to say that Americans are spending more than they should and saving much less than they need to save. As a nation, our sense of thrift seems to have left us and we are no longer a people who possess the attribute of living within our means. "Play now and pain later" is in effect, and we would be much better off as a nation if it were reversed: "pain now and play later."

The Eighth Wonder of the World

There are three dynamics involved in the creation of wealth/retirement funds for the future:
a. How much money will you save/invest monthly and yearly?
b. What will your rate of return be on your money?
c. How many years will your money have, to grow and compound?

Albert Einstein is reputed to have been so impressed with compound interest that he called it the "Eighth Wonder of the World."

Why was a genius such as Einstein so fascinated with something so earthy? Other than cell reproduction, there is probably no other phenomenon on earth that can compare to compound interest. Even then, cell reproduction ends at some point in all animate organisms, whereas compound interest just keeps on replicating, folding in on itself. Think of compounding in terms of a snowball rolling downhill. Since it builds on itself exponentially, the bigger it gets, the bigger it **can** get. The longer a snowball rolls (or the higher up the mountain you start it rolling) the more compounding will expand its size. It works the same way in an investment account that is accruing compound interest. To illustrate, consider the "Christopher Columbus and the Penny" story.

The Power of a Penny

Let's say Christopher Columbus, who as we all know "sailed the ocean blue" in 1492 and discovered the New World, found a penny when he came ashore. And let's say he put the penny in his pocket and, when he returned to civilization, he placed it in an account earning 6% interest. If the explorer had instructed someone to remove the interest every year and put it in a piggybank, the total value collected in that piggybank would eventually accumulate to more than 30 cents. No big deal, right? But, if young Christopher had placed the same penny in an account earning 6% *compounded* interest, and just left it alone, letting the interest earn interest, and then letting that interest earn interest on the interest it earned, what would have happened by the 21st century? That one penny invested in 1492 would have grown to over $121 billion dollars today. Hard to believe? Just get out your calculator and multiply $.01 * 1.06%, and repeat by the number of years since 1492 and see what you come up with.

Are you able to see why it bothers us as financial advisors when we see so many Americans not taking advantage of this economic miracle? They move money out of compound interest accounts cavalierly, without realizing how much they sacrifice by not letting the interest continue compounding. Some investors, perhaps jaded by market volatility and unaware of alternatives, park their money in checking accounts, savings accounts, or stick it in low-paying certificates of deposits. That's like trying to roll that same snowball we mentioned in an earlier paragraph, along a level street instead of allowing it to roll down the mountain and capitalize on the laws of gravity and its own energy.

Financial author and radio talk show host Dave Ramsey tells the story about two men, Ben and Arthur, whose saving patterns vary. Ben started saving $2,000 a year at age 19, stopped saving at age 26, and never saved another dime. His brother, Arthur, started later—at age 27—but saved until age 65, almost his entire life. With a 12% return, guess who came out ahead at retirement? Ben did. He only invested $16,000, but his account grew to $2,288,996 by the time he was 65. By the time Arthur turned 65, his account had grown to $1,532,166. He invested $76,000 over time but never caught up to Ben.

Time and compound interest are the perfect marriage for investment growth. The truth is, few people get wealthy enough to retire comfortably on their wages alone; it just won't happen. But if a young person just starting out can discipline himself or herself to save as little as $50 per month into an account earning as little as 5% compounded interest and keep it up for 40 years, the account will grow to $76,301. The actual amount they carved out of their paycheck would amount to only $24,000, but the interest would amount to $52,301.

Create Your Own Pension

The fact that pensions are being eliminated by corporate America from employee benefit packages these days requires that we create our own. Later on in this book we will cover some of the most popular ways of doing this. A pension, keep in mind, represents *guaranteed* income for life, not *projected* income for life. Since retirement represents *permanent unemployment* for the rest of your life, and since that unemployment could last 20 or 30 years, the earlier you begin saving for this major event in your life, the better off you will be.

SECTION 2

THE MID YEARS
AND YOUR MONEY
(Ages 40-65)

CHAPTER FIVE

In the Accumulation Years, Saving is King

"Money is like manure. You have to spread it around or it smells." - J. Paul Getty

What do the words, "Lark," "Avanti," and "Speedster" have in common? If you know the answer to that, you might be a baby boomer. They were all models of the Studebaker, a car now extinct in America. Studebakers were fast, sleek, dependable, and way ahead of their time. Interestingly, it was the demise of the Studebaker Corporation that started the demise of pensions.

The Studebaker Corporation was named for its founder, John M. Studebaker, who started out making horse-drawn wagons, and began making electric cars in 1902. Models with gasoline engines were added in 1904. In the 1950s Studebakers were known for their futuristic lines and aerodynamic design. The eponymous Studebaker had many "firsts" in the automobile manufacturing world.

They were, for example, the first to install seat belts in the front seat of every car (1963) and the first to make the padded dash a standard feature on all models (1961). It may seem like a small thing now because we take it so much for granted, but in 1946, they were the first auto maker to use "back lighting" on their instrument panels. I suppose you had to turn on the dome light or use a flashlight before then to see how fast you were going or how much fuel you had in your tank.

But none of these things, not even the sleek, powerful Avanti sports car, could rescue the venerable car maker from bankruptcy, and the last Studebaker rolled off the assembly line in 1964. When the bosses began sending the workers home and those same workers began claiming their pension benefits, the accountants started to realize that something was terribly wrong. Because of years of slumping sales, the company's pension plans were so poorly funded they could not afford to keep their pension promises. Thousands of workers had their payouts reduced and some got nothing at all. The workers were understandably angry. They thought their pensions were locked in place and chiseled in stone. When they complained to Congress, their cause was picked up by the UAW (United Auto Workers) union, and the outcry forced Congress to act.

The Employee Retirement Income Security Act, otherwise known as ERISA, was enacted in 1974 in an effort to regulate pension plans. A by-product was a new law that allowed taxpayers to contribute as much as $1,500 per year into something called an "Individual Retirement Account" (IRA).

This was history in the making. Pensions were still viewed as the Holy Grail of retirement income by millions of Americans, but the dam had sprung a leak and what began as a trickle would eventually become a torrent of companies shifting the obligation of caring for retiring workers away from themselves, and onto the individual worker and the federal government. This new law allowing individuals to reduce their taxable income by the amount contributed to an IRA was a boon to self-employed individuals who had no pension. By law, these new IRA accounts were allowed to actually *grow* tax deferred – which meant that you would not have to pay taxes on your money until you withdrew it.

"Was the government crazy?" some savers asked. Yeah, crazy like a fox! Remember, the IRA was not tax *free,* it was tax *deferred.* The Internal Revenue Service would eventually get its share. And by the time the account finished growing and was ready to provide the retiree with withdrawals, the government's share would be much larger than it would have otherwise been. Uncle Sam could afford to be patient, seeing as how he could always print all the money he needed.

Enter the 401(k)

What sounds like a breakfast cereal, or perhaps a vitamin pill, and has virtually replaced the defined benefit pension plan as the foremost retirement vehicle for millions of Americans? If you said 401(k), go to the head of the class.

The 401(k) was not the idea of a senator or congressman. The name comes from section 401(k) of the IRS code that was added in 1978. It was one of those stealth paragraphs added to the law that went unnoticed for a couple of years, until a corporate retirement benefits consultant began to design a plan based on the new law. The consultant's name was Ted Benna.

The new plan would put employees in charge of their own pension plan. The employer, instead of guaranteeing a pay-out, would get a tax break by contributing to the employee's plan. This came to be known as "matching funds," since the employer would match a portion of what the employee contributed. Ironically, the first company for which Benna designed the new plan based on section 401(k) of the IRS code, declined to use it. They felt sure the government would catch on to its potential for lost tax revenue and repeal the new law. The first 401(k) plan began in 1981, and now they have all but replaced pensions. 401(k)s contain more than $3.5 trillion in assets invested in them.

There are pros and cons to the 401(k). On the positive side of the ledger is that the 401(k) puts the employee in charge of his own retirement plan. On the negative side, it is not guaranteed like the former company pensions were. Your contributions are deducted from your pay check. They go to a fund manager, or custodian, such as Vanguard or Fidelity. Typically the custodian uses your contributed funds to buy shares of mutual funds. You may have some voice in how to distribute your funds generically, such as 20% in large cap mutual funds, 30% in small cap mutual funds, 10% in international stocks, and so on. But the actual buying of the shares is done by the fund managers. What happens when the market goes down? Your account value can go down. That is not necessarily the end of the world if you are a young investor, as we will shortly see. But if you are approaching retirement, you do not want your entire nest egg to be at risk.

Dollar-Cost Averaging

When you are a young investor and time is on your side, you can do no wrong. Well, let us qualify that. You can do no wrong if you are plugged into a retirement program, such as an IRA or a 401(k), and you are regular with your contributions to that plan, and if you resist the temptation to pull the money out prematurely.

The invisible force field that surrounds you is called "dollar-cost averaging" and it works like this: Your contributions go to your custodian who then uses the money to buy as many shares of ABC mutual fund as that amount of money can buy. If ABC mutual fund shares *increase* in value, that's wonderful! The value of your account goes up. But what if shares of ABC mutual fund *go down* in value? That's wonderful, too! Why? Because now your money will buy more shares! Those skinny shares will eventually fatten up. Remember, time is on your side because you are young. This is not the case, however, with older folks, as we will see later on in this book.

We cannot say this loudly enough. For dollar cost averaging to work, the investment has to be *continuous.* Make sure you consider your financial ability to continue contributing to your investment strategy over the long haul. This is one of those situations where *time* is way more important than *timing.* If you are enrolled in your employer-sponsored plan, like a 401(k), 457 or 403(b) plan, you don't have to worry about it; you're on "auto pilot." But if you are doing it yourself, you have to make sure that the commitment to continue your contributions is non-negotiable if you want the strategy to work. The idea behind it is, you are *averaging* your investment. You aren't investing too much when the market is high, or too little when the market is low.

"A commitment to an on-going investment strategy may require short-term sacrifices for gains in the long-term. Delayed gratification unfortunately is a concept underutilized by many households today." - *Jon Maxson*

CHAPTER SIX

Evaluating Your Insurance

"Life is what happens to us while we are making other plans" - Allen Saunders

Can you imagine a world without insurance? Oh, sure, you may gripe when you pay the premiums; we all do. But we go ahead and write the check anyway, don't we? Why? Because we know that a number of unfavorable financial consequences can result from an automobile accident. We are acutely aware of the liabilities we incur when we, or one of our family members, get behind the wheel. We could be sued and lose everything we have if the accident is judged to be our fault and the other party is seriously injured. You know of people this has happened to; the thought makes you shiver. You can't put the check in the envelope fast enough. It's the same way with fire insurance, and homeowners insurance. We weigh the cost of the insurance versus the consequences of not having it and conclude that, for the amount it costs to have it, it's far better to have the insurance and not need it, than to need it and not have it.

Insurance is all about pooling the risk. If you have nothing to lose, you need no insurance. The more you have to lose, the more insurance you need. In America, insurance is given special tax treatment under the rules of the Internal Revenue Service so it can also be used as a tool for asset accumulation and income distribution. More on that later. First, a little history on the origins of this financial tool.

History of Insurance

The concept of security in numbers and pooling risk goes back to ancient China and the Middle East. The idea for life insurance was hatched by the Romans in 100 B.C. As grisly as it sounds, the idea began with burial clubs for soldiers who would pay a small amount, in return for the assurance that they would receive a proper burial if they were killed in battle. This was important to them because they believed that if they weren't buried with their ancestors, they ran the risk of being tortured in the afterlife. Fighting Huns and Gauls was dangerous work, but the Romans won most of their battles and more soldiers came back alive than died in battle. This made the cost of belonging to the clubs reasonable and attractive.

As time went by, the idea was expanded to not only pay for burials but to give the soldier's family financial aid if he died in battle. As rudimentary as it was, the details were spelled out in a contract and money was exchanged.

Over the next few hundred years, the burial club idea spread to ordinary citizens. They didn't have a name for it, at least not one that we know of, but according to historians, it was a highly organized and efficient business that produced profits for the club's organizers and administrators. When Rome fell in 476 A.D., the burial clubs vanished.

The concept experienced a rebirth in 1662, when some enterprising Englishmen came up with the first life expectancy tables. John Graunt was the first to compile statistics and predict how long, on average, a person would live in those days. Once human mortality could be calculated to a reasonable degree, companies began springing up to offer contracts to individuals along the lines of the old Roman burial clubs. The first insurance professionals were called "underwriters" because they would write their names under the text of the document that promised to pay a sum of money should the individual named in the document die. Factories were dangerous places, and the memory of the plague was still fresh in the minds of many. These contracts became a popular idea.

In 1759, the Presbyterian Church in Colonial America became the first to offer life insurance when they formed a structure to benefit the families of ministers should they meet with an untimely death. The idea was soon adopted by other religious organizations. What began as a non-profit collective soon became a business, as the concept slowly spread and by 1837, there were over 20 profit-making insurance companies operating, primarily in the northeastern states.

The concept of insurance is much more intricate in its significance today than it was decades ago. While the basic concept is to insure the value of a human life, the business and financial uses for life insurance are many indeed. Some of them include:

Personal Uses

- *Income Replacement* – This is perhaps the most common reason to purchase Life Insurance. The proceeds of a policy can ensure that the insured's beneficiaries receive an income stream like they received before his or her death, and that surviving family members are cared for financially.
- *Settling Personal Debt* – Life insurance can serve to care for the personal and household bills left behind by the deceased.
- *Final Expense* – The proceeds of a life insurance policy can be used to ensure that enough money is left behind to provide for funeral expenses. The average cost of a funeral today is between $6,000 and $10,000.
- *Mortgage Payoff* – Average mortgage debt is estimated at $150,000. Granted, the equity in the property may be sufficient in many cases to pay off the mortgage, but this is only a logical solution when survivors do not need to occupy the home following the death of the owner. Mortgage insurance is usually a term policy purchased independently, or a decreasing term policy sold by the lender and built into the mortgage payments.
- *Charitable, Personal Gifts* – One can use life insurance to make a charitable donation to an organization of one's choice, such as a church or university, or fund a gift to a family member.
- *Education* – Life insurance proceeds can provide for the cost of a college education for one's dependents, the average price of which is hovering around $100,000 for a four-year degree, and rising.

- *Taxes* – Life insurance proceeds may be used to care for federal estate, and state inheritance taxes. Prefunding these obligations preserves the value of the estate.

Commercial Uses

- *Employee Benefits* – Many employers provide group life insurance to employees as part of a benefit package.
- *Business Debt Payoff* – A life insurance policy can be used to pay off a company's debts, in the event of the death of a key individual within the business.
- *Business Protection* – A "key person" life insurance policy can be used to protect a business from the loss of profits, if a key person within the organization should die prematurely. Key person insurance has many uses that can be fully explained by a financial advisor who is licensed in insurance or an insurance professional.
- *Buy-Sell Agreements* – Life insurance can be used to facilitate the continuation of a business' buy/sell agreements, or stock redemption plan, in the event that a partner wishes to buy the business interest of a deceased partner.

Life Insurance as a Retirement Vehicle

Because it is our job, we keep up with both the worlds of Wall Street and insurance, when it comes to concepts and strategies that may help our clients retire with more wealth and fewer headaches. In recent years, we observed several new developments in life insurance

Policies are now designed to grow cash for retirement income. Sure, there have always been "cash growth" policies, or "whole life" policies out there. But we are talking about something entirely new and completely different. These policies may also serve to mitigate risk, but that's not what gets the attention of a financial strategist. Depending on the client's health, age, and other circumstances, these new policies are capable of providing cash for retirement that can often be accessed *tax free.*

Using Life Insurance to Generate Retirement Income

Let's start at the beginning. There are two different types of insurance – **term** and **permanent**, (sometimes called whole life). They have some things in common, but there are significant differences, too. Both term and permanent life insurance require that premium payments be made on a regular basis, in return for a death benefit for the beneficiaries of the insured. But permanent life insurance provides this coverage for as long as the insured lives, and term life insurance is good only for a specific period, such as 10 or 20 years. Permanent life insurance is used to provide cash growth. Term won't do that. Another way to describe the differences is this: term is like renting and permanent is like owning.

There was an insurance revolution of sorts in the early 1980s. Whole life policies offered cash growth, but the rates of return were so low that, when interest rates soared in the late 1970s, it became apparent something was out of whack. Insurance companies were setting arbitrary rates of return, say 1% or 2%. The cost of the insurance was not declared in the policy, so you didn't see what your premium dollar was actually buying you. With savings accounts at the bank yielding double digit returns, many owners of whole life policies were cashing them in to buy much cheaper term policies for the necessary death benefit, and getting their cash growth at the bank. The "buy term and invest the difference" approach to life insurance became fashionable.

The insurance industry, seeing their customers leaving them like rats fleeing a sinking ship, fought back with a new approach – *universal life insurance* (UL). This was permanent life insurance but with a major difference. All the fees, charges, and mortality costs, were transparent, clearly defined in the policy. Also, the interest rate credited to the cash value portion of the policy was based on United States Treasury Bills, which were also returning double digits for a while in the early 1980s.

These new UL policies allowed *flexible premium payments*. The policy holder could pay varying payments over time. Let's say the policy holder was the owner of a business and that business had a good year. The owner could pump additional funds into his policy if he wanted to do that. Why would anyone want to pay more than the proscribed premiums for a life insurance policy? For the ***cash growth!***

These new UL policies also allowed policy holders to make withdrawals from their account at any time. They could take very low-interest loans, as long as they followed the rules of the policy. In essence, then, they could be their own banker. Need to purchase a new car? Borrow the money from your cash account, pay yourself back with interest, and your money continues growing. Unlike retirement programs, where you have to be a certain age to withdraw your money or pay a penalty, these UL policies would allow distributions according to need, not age. Owners of policies controlled when and how they would access their savings.

The greatest advantage of UL policies compared to traditional retirement accounts, however, was the element of tax advantage. Life insurance proceeds are paid to the beneficiary completely income tax-free. If you die owning a retirement account, Uncle Sam has his hand out big time. With baby boomers retiring at the rate of 10,000 per day, strain is being placed on entitlement programs. In the coming decades, the pressure on the federal government to increase taxes will be much greater. What are we getting at? Simply that a ***tax-free*** retirement plan can protect us from that.

The insurance industry is always changing and adapting to meet the demands of the public. When interest rates began to return to normal 6% levels in the late 1980s, some of the luster of Universal Life policies was lost. The stock market began to surge in the 1990s and money once again began to flow into equities. The insurance industry fired back with Index Universal Life, which offered the new IUL policy holders the opportunity to grow their cash predicated on the upward swings of the stock market. When the market turned downward, the account locked in the gains and waited for the next upward swing to continue growing. It was dubbed the "ratchet-reset" feature.

Whether you are a candidate for an index universal life policy may depend on your health, your age, and your financial goals. But here are a few reasons why it makes sense to look at IULs when considering your options:

No negative returns - Anyone who lived through recent stock market volatility, or who owns a t-shirt that says "My Portfolio Survived the Crash of 2008" on the front, understands the value of a guarantee that they will never experience negative returns. IULs do that. If the index used to credit the cash value declines over the period measured, the value does not decline. Unlike qualified plans, there are no caps (limits) on how much money you can save each year. (You are only limited by the size of the policy.) You have a liquid "emergency fund," for life's unexpected events.

The insurance company takes the investment risk - The insurance carrier invests in bonds and index options to provide interest credits to the policy. What happens if one of the bonds defaults? Your contract guarantees you lose nothing. If the counterparty to the index option defaults, like Lehman Brothers did, you don't bear the risk. The insurance company does.

The possibility of higher than average returns - Most safe-money investments also have low yields, as of this writing. One-year CDs (Certificate of Deposits) are returning less than 1%. With IULs, if the index does well over the period measured, then you stand to see some very attractive gains. All of the money you put into a cash value life insurance policy builds tax deferred. You avoid paying income taxes every year, so your money builds faster. Also, unlike qualified plans and annuities, the death benefits and cash values are transferred income tax free to your beneficiaries. Cash value life insurance generally bypasses probate since it is contractually private and involves no public records.

Tax free cash flow in retirement - With IRAs and 401(k)s, you will pay taxes on what you withdraw. IULs can create a totally tax-free retirement cash flow. Through the use of contract loans, the cash flow can be free of federal, state, and local income taxes, as well as free of the alternative minimum tax. This tax-free feature allows the index universal life product to be more attractive than other alternatives, even if those alternatives create a higher pre-tax return. The cash values can be accessed income tax-free, without contractual withdrawal penalties. And, there are no early withdrawal penalties from the Federal Government for withdrawals prior to age 59½. (Not so, with qualified plans or annuities) The cash accumulated in your policy can provide you with a tax-free income in retirement. (Taking withdrawals up to the cost basis and then borrowing the remainder, as long as you keep the policy in-force.) In addition, cash value life insurance is generally not attachable by creditors and cash value life insurance doesn't count as an asset when you apply for college financial aid.

The death benefit - Let's not forget that even though you may be using it for the cash building potential, there is a tax-free death benefit, which can protect a surviving spouse. A policy holder, who uses an IUL to save money for retirement, may be able to stop paying premiums at some point and start taking cash flow as contract loans. The owner can continue to be insured for the rest of his or her life without having to pay additional money into the contract, giving them the protection of life insurance in retirement years, to replace lost pension and social security income at death. It is also noteworthy that many IULs have a disability waiver of premium rider that will pay premiums in the event that the policy holder becomes disabled.

In the interest of presenting both sides of every coin, there are some precautions you need to know regarding using an IUL to save for retirement: We wouldn't call them "downsides" necessarily, or negatives, but before you commit your hard-earned money to any retirement savings strategy, it is wise to know as much as possible about the strategy. These are simply facts you need to know and factor in, when making your decision. Here are some **precautions:**

Buying an IUL is a long-term commitment - The cash value of an IUL will be well below the premiums paid for the first seven years or so. If you don't intend to keep an IUL for 10-15 years, don't buy one. It takes that long for the effect of compound returns to take effect. The mortality costs, and the fees for this type of policy, are paid up front. If you are going to cancel the policy shortly after you purchase it, it's not a wise thing to do. Also, it's not uncommon for an IUL to have surrender charges that last for 10-15 years.

Mortality charges - At its core an IUL is an insurance policy, so there will be mortality charges involved. Don't be shocked when these mortality charges are deducted from the contract value; they will naturally offset some of the interest crediting in the contract, and reduce the net return. If the insured is older, uses tobacco, or has health issues, mortality charges may make purchasing an IUL less attractive because they will eat too far into the cash growth.

Companies can change rates and fees - Most carriers that offer IULs will provide the potential buyer with illustrations to project probable gains in one column and fees and charges in the others. Historically, these rates and charges have been slow to change, but changes have been made from year to year. All these carriers, in the wording of the contracts, reserve the right to make such changes as they feel necessary to maintain profitability. They can increase mortality charges if they choose, or decrease returns by lowering caps.

Letting the contract lapse can be problematic - Too many unpaid loans from the policy could cause it to lapse. If that occurs, the contract holder is taxed on the sum of the cash taken out of the contract, less the premiums that were originally paid. Most carriers have provisions in place to prevent that from happening.

Complexity - Index Universal Life Insurance has more than a few moving parts. You need to know how the machinery works before you invest, which may require that you spend some time with a competent professional who understands and can explain the product.

TEFRA, DEFRA and TAMRA

There was a time when investors could pump as much as they wanted into universal life policies. No more. In 1982, the TEFRA, DEFRA, and TAMRA laws were enacted to prevent the tax advantages of life insurance from being abused. TEFRA stands for *Tax, Equity, Fiscal and Responsibility Act of 1982.* DEFRA stands for Deficit *Reduction Act of 1984 and* TAMRA for *Technical and Miscellaneous Revenue Act of 1988.* Together they outline how a life insurance contract can be funded. Violation of these funding guidelines can cause your universal life insurance contract to become a modified endowment contract (MEC) and it will lose all of the tax benefits associated with life insurance. IULs are considered by the insurance industry to be "investment grade life insurance." It is able to accumulate significant amounts of cash value while still keeping the tax advantages of a life insurance policy.

Among the frequently asked questions about using IULs as a cash growth strategy is, "How safe are they?" After all, they are not insured by the Federal Deposit Insurance Corporation (FDIC), like money in the bank. No insurance product is insured by the FDIC. Insurance companies are required by law to cover at least 100% of their liabilities with reserves, which is why you will hear the term "**100% legal reserve life insurance company**" used when insurance companies are listing their credentials. The government regulates the percentage of an insurance company's capital that can be held in certain assets, which has helped produce an overall record of remarkable safety and solvency. Life insurance and annuities, in fact, are two of the vehicles that can guarantee investment principal while offering minimum growth guarantees for the life of the contract, and of course, all of this is based on the claims paying ability of the insurers.

CHAPTER SEVEN

Solving the Long-Term Care Dilemma

*"We'll show the world we are prosperous, even if we
have to go broke to do it."* - Will Rogers

Since we are on the subject of insurance, we would be remiss if we didn't talk about the white elephant in the room – the real threat of losing all we have built up in our retirement nest eggs because of a health-related life event that we are financially unprepared for. Long-term care insurance, (LTC), has taken a back seat in the focus of many retirement income plans and estate plans and we think we know why. It's something no one wants to think about – going into a nursing home or an assisted living facility. Also, traditional long-term care insurance is (a) expensive and (b) a use it or lose it proposition.

*"**Both of my parents ended up in a nursing home and I can tell you that the cost can be astronomical. You can have a perfect plan of investments put together but if you leave yourself unprotected in this one area, the whole house of cards can come tumbling down. Suddenly you're paying $50,000, $75,000, or $100,000 a year out of your investments for nursing home costs.**"*
– C. Pete Benson

Let's look at a hypothetical, yet typical couple we will call Mark and Mary. They are both 61 years old. After facing the difficult challenges associated with placing Mark's 82-year-old mother into an extended care facility, Mark and Mary began thinking about buying long-term care insurance for themselves. They were shocked to learn that the premiums for a policy could be between $2,000 and $5,000 per year, depending on the level of coverage they selected. The agent told them that, assuming they were both deemed healthy enough to qualify for the coverage, a policy that would provide a total benefit of $164,000 each, based on a daily benefit of $150 for a three-year benefit period, would cost them $4,824 per year. The coverage value of that policy would increase annually because of a 3% inflation option, but that was extra.

"What happens if I die without ever needing the coverage?" Mark asked.

"It's like auto insurance," the agent explained. "If you don't need the coverage, the premiums you pay go into the pool to fund the payout for those who do. That's how insurance works."

"And none of it goes to my wife or my children as a death benefit?"

"No," said the agent. "There is no cash value buildup associated with these types of policies."

"So it's either use it or lose it, right?" Mark asked.

"That's about right," shrugged the insurance agent.

Another hypothetical yet typical person, let's call her Brenda, purchased long-term care insurance at age 54. She had read articles that said the cost of assisted living care and in-home nursing care was rising at double the rate of inflation. She did have some savings and a small pension, but a year's stay in a nursing home would just about wipe her out. She figured that since she was relatively healthy, and relatively young, she would be able to afford the premiums. Fifteen years later, however, at age 67, Brenda got a letter from her LTC insurance carrier telling her that her $200 monthly premium would be going up to $370 per month; almost double! Now she faced a real dilemma. She couldn't afford to drop the policy, or keep it either. If she dropped it, everything she paid into it was down the proverbial black hole. Her agent explained to her that she could reduce the benefits by increasing the elimination period, or the wait period – the length of time during which the stay was not covered. She could also reduce the time period for which the policy would cover her if her stay was protracted. What a difficult choice Brenda had to make, but it was one in which she couldn't avoid. Sadly, Brenda, Mark and Mary are not alone. All across America, millions of people are faced with the same dilemma – can't afford to have it and can't afford not to.

Insurance companies are also feeling the pinch. According to an article that appeared in the <u>Chicago Tribune</u>'s business section on April 13, 2012, entitled "Long Term Care Dilemma," Reuters correspondent Kathleen Kingsbury reported that the two pronged problem of an aging population and the rising cost of health care was putting insurance companies in a difficult position, with 10 out of the top 20 carriers in the country leaving the market in the last five years. She reported that prices on new long-term care plans were 6% to 17% higher than comparable coverage of the previous year. Some providers, she said, were seeking approval for premium increases of as high as 90%.

With the use-it-or-lose-it terms of these policies and their skyrocketing premiums, it is no wonder many are simply saying "no, thank you" to long-term care insurance. The insurance carriers contend they are merely adjusting to the reality of the situation. They point out that the low-interest rate environment that prevails at the time of this writing makes it more difficult for them to manage the investment pools from which claims are paid.

"The long-term care industry is still young and only now is seeing actual usage data, which indicates the need for rate increases," read a statement by John Hancock Financial, one of the largest providers still selling LTC policies.

According to the U.S. Department of Health and Human Services, some 70% of people over 65 will require long-term care of some kind during their lifetime, at a cost ranging from $4,000 to $8,000 per month, and persons with more than $2,000 in assets can't qualify for Medicaid assistance. According to the *Genworth 2013 Cost of Care Survey,* the average price of a semi-private room in a nursing home is $207 per day nationwide, and $183 per day in Tennessee. You will pay a bit more for a private room and costs vary from city to city, but not much. Long story short, plan on paying at least $70,000 per year, and that cost is likely to increase by 4% to 5% over the next five years. According to Kiplinger, the average nursing home stay lasts 2.4 years.

Sad to say, but the patients will never return to an active life once they are admitted.

Wait a minute. Doesn't Medicare cover any of that?

Medicare will only pay for 100 days in a nursing home, and the rough equivalent for home health care. But Medicare rules stipulate that the payment is only for the time you are receiving what is called "skilled care," which is defined as around-the-clock care needed for a patient to "continue to improve." The phrase "continue to improve" is the determining factor as to whether you even receive the 100 days of care. For example, if you are receiving rehabilitation therapy after surgery, Medicare will cover the cost as long as the rehab is needed *if* you are still improving. As soon as the doctors deem you to have reached a plateau in your recovery, even if it is merely a pause in the process, then you are technically no longer "continuing to improve" and Medicare stops paying – whether you have been receiving the therapy for 20 or 90 days.

So, no, Medicare doesn't pay for long term health care, not really. If you do not have long-term care insurance, and you can't afford private pay, that leaves Medicaid.

How Medicaid Works

According to some published estimates, 7 out of 10 people in nursing homes are on Medicaid. Although Medicaid was created to pay for health care for the poor, many recipients of Medicaid benefits are middle-class folks who burned through their savings first, and then, when they qualified for pauper status under the government's guidelines, became dependent on the government for their care.

Some of these people may have been contributing members of society, business owners and entrepreneurs, taxpayers, and property owners, at one time. But they were reduced to indigent status either by high medical costs prior to their entering the nursing home, or by the high costs charged by the facility once they were there.

Some choose to adjust their net worth before they become ill so they can qualify for Medicaid when the time comes. How? By getting rid of their assets, perhaps giving them away to their children, so they can fit the government's Medicaid criteria. There is nothing illegal about this but it is not always easy to do. First of all, Uncle Sam knows this is done, so he has inserted some complications to the process. Any adjustment to your finances with this in mind must follow the strict rules the government has imposed. There is what is called a ***"five-year look back,"*** which is strictly enforced. It is specifically designed to prevent those above the eligibility levels for Medicaid from giving away their resources at the last minute, just so they can qualify for nursing home care under Medicaid.

Medicaid is a federally funded, state administered program. The State of Tennessee's Medicaid program is known as TennCare, an agency that provides health care for 1.2 million Tennesseans. In 2013, TennCare's annual budget was approximately $9 billion. At any time during this five-year look-back period, the state can audit the books of anyone who is receiving benefits to determine if any assets, including real property, cash, or any other form of assets, have been transferred out of the name of the person receiving benefits. These examiners will be looking for anything of value that was given away to children or grandchildren. They especially look for gifts of money, even if they are designated as money to pay for education. Gifts of property, such as a car or a house, will not be allowed unless the recipient of the gift paid full market value in return. If that is not the case, then the amount transferred will be disallowed, and not considered when calculating Medicaid eligibility.

Some think that because the IRS allows you to gift $14,000 per year to family members that this is outside the scope of the Medicaid audit. No, it counts. We have found that in dealing with the government on these matters, saying, "I didn't know," or "I forgot" doesn't work. It is best to seek the advice of an elder-law attorney, or a competent planning specialist, when you are in this zone.

Many are also not aware of some of the changes that came about as a result of the passage of the Deficit Reduction Act of 2005 (DRA). This dramatically changed the qualifications for Medicaid-funded nursing home care. It is imperative to plan properly with these new rules in mind. Before the DRA became law, the look-back period was three years instead of five years. The use of irrevocable trusts can be useful in this regard, but a trust that is improperly structured is like a boat with leaks; it will not float for very long when the time comes to use it.

Anyone who has been through this process will understand what the term "spend down" means. An applicant who is close to qualifying for Medicaid, but not there yet, must use up his financial assets on the list of items allowed. If the money is spent on items ***not*** on the "spend down" list, then the expenditure will be subject to the look-back. Approved "spend down" categories include such things as pre-paying funeral expenses, and replacing an old automobile. But the list is clearly defined and you will need to examine it carefully, preferably with the help of a professional. The process can be very painful as well as tricky.

Possible New Solutions

Insurance companies are in business to make a profit. When long-term care insurance first began to be developed in the 1970s, it was reasonable and affordable. That was before government regulation forced facilities to improve on the level of their care, which led to increased costs and higher premiums, which led to many declining to buy it. Consequently, many of the carriers who sold traditional long-term care insurance left the market. But since free enterprise abhors a vacuum, the insurance industry began searching for new ways to market policies that would allow them to fill a need for long-term care coverage and still make a profit. Some of these new approaches are quite innovative. Here are a few in brief form:

Combos – This is a hybrid product, hence the word "combo," which is short for "combination policies", that combine aspects of a traditional fixed annuity with aspects of long-term care coverage. The fixed annuity portion of the contract provides a guaranteed interest rate that is usually more than double, if not triple, what a bank certificate of deposit would earn. The other side of the "combo" is a long-term care coverage that would pay out two to three times the initial policy value over two or three years, after the annuity account value is depleted.

For example, a purchaser of a $100,000 annuity who had selected a benefit limit of 300%, and a two-year long-term care benefit factor, would have an additional $200,000 available for long-term care expenses, even after the initial $100,000 annuity policy value was depleted. The policy owner would spend down the annuity value over a two-year period and then receive the additional $200,000 over a four-year period, or longer. In other words, an annuity purchased with $100,000 could potentially payout LTC benefits of $300,000. In that respect, then, it is a fixed annuity and long-term care coverage combined. This product requires a significant, up-front deposit, usually at least $100,000, to make it strong enough to adequately cover health care costs.

Although it has a few more moving parts, it is worth a look. A provision made possible by the Pension Protection Act of 2006, now makes it possible to pay for long-term care benefits from an annuity tax-free. This new approach solves a problem, but it is not for everybody. We recommend you see a competent retirement planning specialist who is up to date on these contracts, so you can examine their suitability for you. Also, while they do not involve the strict underwriting of the traditional long-term care insurance policies, there is some underwriting involved. In other words, poor health may disqualify you.

Life Insurance/LTC Combos - To make it simple, the annuity/LTC combo is usually used by those who are in good health and who are age 60 and above with some cash to invest. The insurance industry has also designed life insurance policies with long term care riders. These are becoming popular with those who are under age 60 and in relatively good health. The reason is; life insurance premiums get higher as you get older. You usually buy these policies with a lump sum deposit called a "single premium." Like the annuity combo, the premium is usually one-third to one-half of the death benefit. The long-term care benefit is usually around 2% of the death benefit per month.

Here's an example. John buys a life insurance/LTC combination policy and pays a $50,000 premium for a $100,000 death benefit and a long-term care rider. The cash value (not the *surrender* value) is approximately $50,000. The long-term care benefit would be approximately $2,000 per month if needed. One important caveat: whatever money is paid out in long-term-care benefits, reduces the policy's cash value by that same amount. Again, this approach is not for everyone and there is a degree of complexity to these solutions. But we think they offer a more attractive solution to the LTC cost and coverage problem than does traditional long-term care insurance.

Usually we are reluctant to come right out and endorse something, but we have looked at these combination policies with a pretty powerful microscope and we can't see any significant flaws in them. If you have lived any time at all in the adult world, then you know nothing is perfect and nothing is free. But with these policies, the buyer will get some benefit from premiums even if he or she doesn't eventually need long term care. The expression "win-win situation" has been overused, but we think it applies here. Either you use some, or all, of the long-term care benefits or *someone* receives a life insurance payment, or you enjoy the proceeds of the annuity growth, or you pass it along to your beneficiaries.

Not All Policies Are the Same

As with all things financial, you don't want to rush headlong into any strategy, policy, plan, or investment, without first taking the time to make a thorough investigation and make sure you understand it. Are all combination policies the same? No. Not all insurance companies are the same. Check the ratings, such as those provided by A.M. Best, Moody's, Standard and Poors, or Fitch, for example. These are independent evaluations of an insurance company's financial soundness. Remember too, that's *all* they are. They do not measure the company's willingness or capability when it comes to handling claims. Nor do ratings measure the level of customer service. They are not the end-all measure by which to assess an insurance company, but they are statistically-driven indicators that should be looked at when making a decision.

Next, there are the actual benefits versus premium comparison. Here is a real comparison provided by the American Association for Long Term Care Insurance of two policies from two leading insurance companies. In each case, analysts compared policies for a 65-year-old married female. The initial policy required a $100,000 single payment.

Policy A would pay a Death Benefit of **$193,906** and a monthly long-term care benefit of **$8,079.**

Policy B would pay a Death Benefit of **$150,121** and a monthly long-term care benefit of **$6,255.**

Policy C would pay a Death Benefit of **$165,997** and a monthly long-term care benefit of **$5,533.**

Those differences are significant, so it pays to seek the help of a professional who knows how the gears work in these products, and can make sure you get the most in the way of benefits for every dollar paid in premium.

Some Things to Think About

We make these points, not to persuade anyone to buy anything; that's not what we are about at all. But it pains us to see all the good planning one can do come to nothing, because one link in the planning chain was weak. Our job is to find solutions to prevent that. What you do regarding those solutions is up to you.

In all of this, the statistic that continues to jump out at us is the one that says 7 out of 10 Americans will land in a nursing home sometime after 65. If you went to the airport, ready to take off on a vacation trip, and the airline people informed you that 7 out of the next 10 planes were not going to make it to their destinations, but would have to make an emergency landing somewhere that would cost you time and money...or worse yet, crash...would you even consider using that airline? And yet people take chances with their assets and their health in such a manner, by ignoring consequences of not making at least some effort to prevent the cost of long-term care from eating up their hard-earned assets.

Consider these three factors when deciding what to do about LTC coverage:

Your Assets – Do you need $150,000 in coverage on your automobile insurance policy if you drive a Yugo? No. (We are safe in using the Yugo because (a) they don't make them anymore and (b) Yugoslavia, the country where they were made, is no longer a country.) You buy a policy that is adequate to cover the assets you wish to protect. If you don't own a home, have a substantial income, or own investments of any kind, then you may be a candidate for Medicaid, if they don't change the rules by the time you need the care.

Your current health – Insurance companies will only issue you a policy if you are, at the time of the application, relatively healthy. That may seem obvious enough, but you would be surprised how many times we get calls to our office from someone wanting to purchase LTCI right after they have received bad news from their doctors. Usually, by that time, it's too late. Underwriters are getting stricter, too. If you battle such things as weight issues, high blood pressure, or arthritis, you are a question mark.

Your age – Simply put, the younger you are, the less it costs. Look for a company with a good track record on not raising rates. Know also that there are creative ways to pay your premiums, including employee benefits, and paid up plans designed to take care of the whole balance in a 10-year period.

The easiest way to know if you are a candidate for long-term care insurance is to imagine how you would pay for your care if you needed it this very second. If the cost was, for example, $7,000 per month, how much of your personal assets could you afford to put towards that? If the answer is $4000, then you could get a policy to cover the remaining $3,000. Some who are extremely wealthy aren't candidates for long-term care insurance. If they need long-term care they can use their own assets to pay for it, without affecting their lifestyle. For the average, middle-class American, however, $7,000 per month flowing out of a non-renewable resource pool could soon impoverish them.

Many want to know how to stay out of a nursing home and, in the event of an accident or illness, be able to stay in their own homes for as long as possible. Ask your financial professional about strategies that will cover you but won't leave you paying premiums you cannot afford.

Would you believe that some financial planners have been sued for malfeasance, because they failed to point out the need for some type of LTC coverage? In some cases, children of parents who lost all their wealth due to nursing home expenses, have taken legal action against the planner, accusing them of not covering this contingency in their planning sessions. This is one reason why we always make notes in the client file confirming that we have reviewed LTC options. We acknowledge that long-term care planning can be a tedious and annoying process. It requires decisions and can cost money that we can always find a use for elsewhere. But it may be one of the most prudent estate planning steps you will ever take.

CHAPTER EIGHT

Looming Threats to Your Financial Security

"The best time to plant an oak tree is 20 years ago;
the next best time is now."
- David Chilton, in *The Wealthy Barber*

Some of you who are reading this book may be old enough to remember the late 1970s and early 1980s, when James Earl Carter was president, the mini skirt was high fashion, and men sported flashy polyester "leisure suits" with bell-bottom trousers. That time was also marked by a brief period of double-digit inflation. Interest rates jumped through the roof – on both the borrowing end and the savings end – and so did prices.

In those days, certificates of deposit were returning 15%. It was a fantastic rate of return, true. But what good was it if roaring inflation and higher taxes were eating your account up from the other end? Once you added up the positives and the negatives, you were going in the hole.

There is an old saying attributed to George Santayana: "Those who cannot remember the past are condemned to repeat it." As we write this, Inflation is relatively tame, averaging between 2.5% and 3% per year. The inflation monster that reared its ugly head in the Jimmy Carter era has been caged now for decades. Could it happen again? What causes runaway inflation, anyway?

What Causes Inflation?

When the 36th U.S. President, Lyndon B. Johnson, took office after the assassination of John F. Kennedy, he had some big shoes to fill politically. Johnson burned the fiscal candle at both ends to raise money *for his War on Poverty and The Great Society*, not to mention the Vietnam War. All this drained the treasury at an alarming rate. When President Richard M. Nixon was sworn in on January 20, 1969, as the nation's 37th president, he inherited a recession from his predecessor. Nixon, always the crafty politician, knew he couldn't stop the spending spree if he intended to be re-elected for a second term in the 1972 election – at least not until the election was over. But natural economic forces were at work that couldn't be stopped. To quell them, Nixon imposed wage and price controls in 1971. These controls gave the appearance of working through the election year that followed, but it was like the lid on an inflation pressure cooker; eventually it would explode. Once those measures to contain the upward movement of wages and prices were removed, those two pistons, wage and price, that define the economy, made up for lost time. Once begun, it was like a horse race, neck and neck down the stretch. Prices surged ahead; wages caught up and passed. Prices came from behind to overtake wages, and so on, and so on.

The Federal Government is the only entity in our democratic society that has the authority to print money. In order to print more and more money (which nearly always fuels inflation) Nixon had to break the last link connecting American currency to gold. This led to a devaluation of the American dollar. It was like dousing a fire with lighter fluid. Interest rates that had been kept artificially low by the Federal Reserve began to rise after the 1972 election year.

One of the most defining books on this era is William Greider's *Secrets of the Temple: How the Federal Reserve Runs The Country.* Greider quoted Nixon as follows: "We'll take inflation if necessary, but we can't take unemployment." When the president was forced to resign in 1974 as a result of the Watergate investigation, inflation had risen from 3.6% to 9.4%, and by the fall of 1974 it was at 12%. Some remember when President Gerald Ford, the 38th president, vowed to "WIN" the war on inflation, which he declared was "public enemy number one." WIN stood for Whip Inflation Now and buttons bearing the clever logo were sported by members of both

50

congressional parties in support. The buttons did little good. Critics of the program began wearing the buttons upside down, claiming that NIM stood for "Need Immediate Money."

By the time James Earl Carter was sworn in as the 39th president, the die was cast. Inflation would peak at 14.76% in March, 1980. The domino effect was inevitable. Average Americans couldn't afford to borrow money for a car or a house. New homes sat empty and auto dealerships closed. Ironically, the only cure for inflation was the recession that the hyperinflation had caused in the first place, which proved once again that, in a free market economy, the ship will right itself if left alone. It is when the government interferes too much with the free enterprise system, that things go haywire.

Financial Planning and Inflation

Some doom-and-gloom prophets warn of a return of double digit inflation, but the Fed does seem to have learned some lessons from the past. Hopefully those lessons will not soon be forgotten. From a financial planning standpoint, it is wise to figure on a constant annual  inflation rate of 3%. Why that number? When you go to the early 1900s and calculate it, the nation's average inflation rate comes in at just above 3%. Yes, that includes the wild and wooly Jimmy Carter days, as well as the times we actually experienced deflation in the Great Depression.

The thing about inflation is that at 3%, the effects are difficult to see in the short run; you have to get the long view to appreciate it. For example, the price of a gallon of gasoline will fluctuate a few cents over a few years. But if you look at it from 1960, when it was 29 cents per gallon, to currently, when it is bouncing around $3.50 per gallon, you can see the effects of inflation clearly. In 1960, the average cost of a house was approximately $12,000. By 2014 you paid that for a used car! A house that cost $25,000 in 1960 sells for $170,000 today.

So what will the cost of living be 20 years from now? Thirty years from now? According to research performed by the Society of Actuaries (SOA), only 72% of pre-retirees, and 55% of retirees, have calculated the effects of inflation on their retirement plan. Ten years into their retirement, however, they will be spending $13 to buy what $10 buys today. In 20 years, they will be spending $18 to buy what $10 will buy today.

So what are some ways to take inflation into account when planning for retirement?

1. One of the best ways to address the risk of inflation is to delay your Social Security, if possible, to age 70. Doing so, experts suggest, will give you the highest possible, inflation-adjusted, guaranteed stream of income from Social Security. Depending on your age, you could increase your annual benefit up to 8% percent per year.

2. Consider also investing in an immediate income annuity with an inflation rider. Income annuities are insurance contracts purchased with a single lump sum that offer immediate income payments (usually monthly) for a specified period, or for the annuitant's lifetime.

3. Ask your retirement income planning specialist about fixed-indexed annuities with income riders. These insurance products are designed to guarantee safety of principal and provide an income that you can't outlive. If you know how much you *have* to invest, and you know how long you can defer the account before accessing the funds, you can accurately predict to the dollar how much your guaranteed lifetime income will be.

In fact, while you are at it, go ahead and ask your retirement planning specialist the hard questions: "If I want to retire at age 65, how much adjusted-for-inflation income will I need, and how much will I have to have saved in order to accomplish that?" A competent advisor will be able to answer the question. When making retirement plans, there is no way to cover all possible scenarios, or deal with all possible contingencies. But it is only prudent to build into a strategy the extra money that will, in all probability, be needed to compensate for 3% inflation. If that requires living on a budget now so we will not have to scrimp later, then so be it. If it means working longer so we can hit our magic number in retirement, it would be prudent to do so.

SECTION 3

YOUR RETIREMENT YEARS
(Age 65 and beyond)

CHAPTER NINE

Will the "Golden Years" Be Golden?

"Money isn't the most important thing in life, but it's reasonably close to oxygen on the 'gotta have it' scale." -Zig Ziglar

One reason why retirement is called "The Golden Years" is because, by the time the 60s and 70s roll around, we should have accumulated a degree of wealth, which is associated with gold. The phrase "Golden Years" also reminds us of those long, golden, summer afternoons, when the working hours of the day are over and we can relax and enjoy ourselves. The "Golden Years" are, finally, for us, a time to follow our dreams, do whatever it is that we want to do, when we want to do it. Do absolutely nothing if we want to. Or play 36 holes of golf each day if that is our vice, or fish, or play with the grandkids. You get the idea.

But all that goes so much better with adequate funds at our disposal. Author and motivational speaker Zig Ziglar made a good point in the quote above. How true that statement is in our golden years.

But according to the 2013 Retirement Confidence Survey, conducted by the Employee Benefit Research Institute, only 28% of American workers are confident about having enough money for a comfortable retirement. Why do you suppose that is?

The economy is showing signs of vigor and recovery, after taking a knockout blow in the 2008 market crash, and receiving some vicious kicks to the midsection during the subsequent recession. The EBRI suggests the growing lack of confidence is because people are waking up to just how much they need to save for retirement, and how little they have actually saved. Before the market crash of 2008, some were apparently lulled into a sense of complacency, projecting that their retirement account balances would continue to grow. For many, the shock of losing 30-50% of their life's savings was a big wake up call.

"Asked how much they believe they will need to save to achieve a financially secure retirement, a striking number of workers cite large savings targets: 20 percent say they need to save between 20 and 29 percent of their income and nearly one-quarter (23 percent) indicate they need to save 30 percent or more," the survey revealed.

For most people, those savings targets are unrealistic. That is why a large number of workers don't even try to reach them. Another startling fact the report revealed was how few people plan for retirement or seek professional help. "Only 46 percent report they and/or their spouse have tried to calculate how much money they will need to have saved by the time they retire so that they can live comfortably in retirement," the report stated. How many retirees reported having obtained advice from a professional financial advisor? Only 28%!

Why Do So Few Plan for Retirement?

From our point of view, failing to seek financial advice when needed is like failing to seek medical advice for a physical ailment. One is hazardous to your health, and the other is hazardous to your wealth. There is an adage that seems to fit here: There are three types of people: Those who make things happen, those who watch things happen, and those who say, "What happened?" If there is one message we want to convey in *Money Enough for Life?* it is that you must take charge of your future by making plans.

Failing to plan is simply not an option. In fact, failing to plan is the same as *planning* to fail. So why is it that most people will spend days planning a vacation but give so little attention to this important phase of their life? There are several reasons:

1. "I'm just so confused by all the conflicting advice." – Few things are as frustrating as being lost, asking for directions, and receiving conflicting advice. These days we are inundated by investment advice. Have you noticed how many financial magazines there are these days? They compete for our attention with sensational headlines: "Buy Gold Now Before It's Too Late," shouts one. "Why The Gold Rush Is Over" screams another. The cable networks feature several financial channels with producers pitting bickering analysts against each other, with a moderator who plays referee. It may be good television but it fails to guide us in a meaningful way. Most bizarre is the loud talking fellow who comes on wearing a party hat and gives us stock-buying tips to the sound of zoom whistles and bulb horns. Are we really meant to take such clownish behavior seriously? Perhaps not, but many do.

> *"It is so very sad that families early on don't begin working with a Wealth Planner to design their financial plan through the rest of their life. Failing to plan is simply not an option."*
> *–C. Pete Benson*

Probably the worst financial advice comes from those with the best intentions – our friends and relatives. Uncle Fred can't wait to whisper his "hot stock tip" in our ear at family reunions. Brother Bob thinks he has found the next *Google* and we should "get in now while the getting is good."

Then there is the conflicting advice that comes from professionals whose investing philosophies are diametrically opposed. It is not unusual for professional people to disagree. Conflicting opinions in the medical field are so commonplace that most insurance companies require a second opinion before authorizing a costly procedure. For example, a person with back pain who visits a surgeon may hear a much different treatment recommendation than one who visits an osteopath. In some cases, there is no one right solution to a medical problem; there may be several approaches that work.

In the financial advisory world there are proponents of a strictly market-based approach to retirement planning. Then there are the advisors who believe insurance products, such as annuities, are the only answer to every problem. Both may be fully-trained and fully-certified professionals with degrees and certifications to match, but they are separated 180 degrees by their different investing philosophies. Why is that? Most likely because they received their training from different schools of thought. As Abraham Maslow said, "To one who only has a hammer, every problem looks like a nail." In our experience, the solution is seldom found on the poles but on the equator. In other words, the truth between two extreme opinions is often in the middle.

2. "The government will take care of me." – No, it won't. Social security is set up to help people when they reach retirement age, but unless you are willing to live near the poverty line, you will need to supplement your Social Security. According to the Social Security Administration, in 2013 almost 58 million Americans received some $816 billion in Social Security benefits. The average monthly Social Security check totaled $1,269, or a little over $15,000 annually. The maximum Social Security benefit in 2013 was $30,396 per year.

You have probably contributed to the Social Security fund for years, but will you be able to reap the benefits? We are not on the doom-and-gloom band wagon with those who warn of the imminent demise of Social Security. Baby boomers (those born between 1946 and 1964) should have no problem collecting their benefits. Those born after 1964? The best we can give them is a hand waggle. We believe some changes must be made to the system if it is to continue. Even the Social Security Administration acknowledges this. Scary headlines about the depletion of the Social Security program have been in the news for years. Note the grim text of a warning that appears on yearly statements sent to future Social Security recipients, informing them that unless changes are made, the Social Security Trust Fund will be exhausted by 2033:

> Without changes, in 2033 the Social Security Trust Fund will be able to pay only 75 cents for each dollar of scheduled benefits. We need to resolve these issues soon to make sure Social Security continues to provide a foundation of protection for future generations.

3. "It's too soon to plan for retirement." – It is never too soon to start planning and making decisions to help you become financially secure in retirement. Procrastinating in this area makes the savings bar too high to reach later on. Our advice is to start planning for your retirement as soon as you start earning. Make it a habit to save at least 10% of your gross salary. Avoid debt like the plague. If you find yourself in debt, tighten your belt and pay it off. As Suze Orman says, "Live below your means but within your needs." And as American philosopher, Bill Earle, so wittily expressed it: "If your outgo exceeds your income, then your upkeep will be your downfall."

It may be true that in the early years of working, retirement seems an eternity away. And for most people, starting salaries don't allow much room for savings. But time is your biggest asset when you are young. The power of compounding is so huge (see chapter four) that even if you can only save one or two percent of what you earn, you will love yourself later for doing it. This is the surest way to financial independence, and it is never too soon to start that process.

Believe it or not, we hear the "too soon to plan" excuse from some who are in their 50s and early 60s. We encourage them to at least take stock and see where they are. We have actually sat down with some individuals and helped them write out their goals. In our experience, most people have goals; they just haven't articulated them. Our suggestion is to put those objectives, goals, whatever you want to call them, under a microscope. Sort through them like you would the contents of your closet. Which ones are reasonable and achievable at this point in your life? Keep those, just like you would the clothes in your closet you can still wear. Toss out what is unachievable and work on what's left.

While we're on the subject of goals, in our *pro bono* financial workshops, we make the point that, for a goal to work for you, it has to have the following characteristics:

Specific – Not "I want to lose weight," but "I want to lose 10 pounds." Not "I want to retire comfortably," but, "I want to retire with an annual income of $60,000, not including my Social Security."

Achievable – It's okay to dream, but separate dreams from your goals. Goals are not fanciful things. They are work engines to success. You must be able to get a clear vision of something actually happening before it can make your goal list.

Measurable – Break your goals down into bite-size accomplishments. For example, to use the weight loss example again: "I will lose one pound in the next eight days." Another Ziglar quote we love is, "By the inch it's a cinch; by the mile it's a trial." Money goals should have a deadline, too. Now your goals have "legs" as the expression goes. Your savings goal should likewise be specific.

Written – When it's in writing, it takes on the power of a contract; treat it like one. Sign it, and keep it where you can refer to it often and track your progress. You will fare so much better if, every year, you set your annual financial goals based on your written values. If you have procrastinated up until now in this endeavor, it's not too late to start. Naturally, the sooner you start, the better; but work with the time you have left.

4. "It's too late for me to plan for retirement." – It is never too late! There might be options available to you of which you are unaware. Income generating strategies are constantly evolving and there might be a strategy which you have not yet considered. For example:

- If you got behind in your savings, for example, you may be able to play "catch up." The maximum amount of contributions a person can make to his or her 401(k) plan is set each year by the IRS. For 2014, the maximum was $17,500. But if you are 50 or older, you can chunk in an additional $5,500, so you may be able to go into "power-savings mode" with tax-deferred contributions of up to $23,000.

- Is your employer matching your contributions? Sweet! Elective deferrals are treated separately from the employer's matching contributions. Even though employer match contributions are limited to 25% of your salary (or 20% of your net self-employment income if you are self-employed), you could have elective salary deferral plus employer matching contributions of up to $52,000 for the year 2014. That is catch up in high gear!

If you are starting late, develop the mindset that you can't do anything about yesterday or the year before. Those trains have left the station. Focus on tomorrow. Begin by making some serious decisions and assess what your income streams are going to look like after you collect that final paycheck. How can you make the most out of your present situation? Amongst the biggest decisions is when to take Social Security benefits so as to maximize your payout.

We touched on this a little in the previous chapter, but as everyone knows, the earlier you start collecting your Social Security, the smaller is the amount of your monthly check. Every situation is different, so it is wise to consult with a financial advisor who specializes in retirement income planning, for the specifics as they relate to your individual case. The advisor should be able to help you weigh both levels of retirement benefits when alive, and any survivor benefits that are applicable after the death of a spouse.

That having been said, however, it is generally correct to say that, if a single person is in good health and is not in dire need of Social Security income, it makes sense to wait as long as possible to begin collecting it. Why? Because for every year you delay taking full benefits, your eventual Social Security payout will go up by as much as 8%. There is always the temptation to begin collecting Social Security just because it's there. But when you compare that guaranteed 8% on a lifetime income to any investment available on the private market today, it's hard to beat it.

For couples, it's better for higher earners to delay taking Social Security as long as possible. That will boost their payouts while they are alive and, under Social Security's rules, after one spouse dies, the surviving spouse receives the higher of the two benefits.

5. "My finances are in such a mess, I don't know where to start." – This one reminds us of those people who spend hours tidying up, because they don't want the people they have hired to clean their home see what a mess they have. Relax. If you don't know where to start, your financial advisor can show you. You aren't the first person who has come through the doors of Beacon Capital Management with a mess, and we seriously doubt you will be the last.

Some people are like ostriches when it comes to planning their financial futures. It hurts their heads to think about something as detailed and involved as they imagine financial planning to be, so they close their eyes, hoping it will fix itself. For example, we know of individuals who have had several jobs over the last couple of decades and have multiple 401(k) accounts. Their accounts are scattered here, there, and everywhere to the point that they have only a vague idea of where their money is and don't know why it's there.

Taking the first step to simplifying your financial life may help eliminate some of this stress. A proper financial plan helps you organize your finances and also provides a track for you to follow. Even if you have a plan in place, it is prudent to review it on a regular basis. Get a second opinion if it doesn't seem to be working for you.

CHAPTER TEN

Adjusting Your Risk Tolerance in the Red Zone of Retirement

"Almost any man knows how to earn money,
but not one in a million knows how to spend it."
- Henry David Thoreau

In football, the "red zone" is the area of the field between the 20-yard line and the goal line. When a team is on offense and has the ball in the red zone, the game changes for them. They have less room in which to operate. They must exercise more caution because the defense has less ground to cover.

Quarterbacks may pass the ball in the end zone, but they must be very accurate with their throws. An interception here and any scoring opportunities are lost, and the ball will be turned over to the other team. Runners are coached to tuck the balls under their arms when they run, gripping them ever tighter the closer they are to the goal line.

Buffet Rule

Rule #1: Never lose money.
Rule #2: Never forget Rule #1.

A fumble also ends all scoring opportunities.

The critical years just before and just after retirement have often been compared to the football red zone. It is a time when money left in the stock market is vulnerable. A sudden correction could cause a person to fumble the ball and lose a significant portion of his or her life savings.

It goes without saying that the "red zone" is the area of the financial playing field where you want to be wise, not foolish, with your investment choices. The resources you are "playing with," so to speak, are in large measure non-renewable. To continue the football analogy, the game clock is winding down. If it were early in the game, you could recover from losses incurred here. But this is the fourth quarter and caution should be your watchword.

Reverse Dollar Cost Averaging

For instance, let's say we have a 64-year-old female who wishes to retire next year. She has no pension, but does have $400,000 in her 401(k). She wants to produce a secure income to augment her Social Security. You are her financial coach; what is your advice? Leave it with the company where she works and leave the money invested in 401(k)s? To continue with the football analogy, that's tantamount to lobbing a "Hail Mary" (a dangerous pass you pray will be caught for a touchdown) to a receiver you hope will grab the ball. And yet, that is what some retirees do because they don't know they have other options.

What got you TO retirement is not the vehicle you want to get you THROUGH retirement.

In chapter five we covered the principle of dollar cost averaging, and how that principle helped you steadily build wealth in your 401(k) account. You contributed the same amount each paycheck. Because you had time and were consistent, you couldn't be hurt by market volatility. If the market was up, your account rose with it; if the market was down, your contribution bought more shares that would later increase in value. It was a win/win situation for you. That was the vehicle that got you *to* retirement. The mistake many make is figuring they can continue using that same vehicle to get them *through* retirement. But think about it for a moment and you will see why investing after you retire the same way you did before you retired is a recipe for disaster.

Why? Because what was once a regular *contribution* to the account, now becomes your regular *withdrawal.* If you depend on this account to help you meet your day-to-day expenses, then you must withdraw the same amount each month. Each time you make a withdrawal, you are selling shares. Can you adjust the size of the withdrawal to accommodate the swings in the market? No. When shares are lower in value, you simply sell more of them. Earlier, when you were contributing to the account, there were no worries about this market fluctuation. Now that shares are being removed from the account, you cannot take advantage of a recovering market. Those shares, once they are gone, are gone forever. Time, which was once your friend, is not working against you; the process is reversed. You are a victim of reverse dollar cost averaging.

Although that may be as obvious to you as the noonday sun, we are constantly amazed at the millions of Americans who leave their retirement accounts at risk in the market and with their former employer. A 2010 survey conducted by ING Direct USA, shows nearly a quarter of the 50% of workers who reported having an orphaned 401(k) left between $10,000 and $50,000 in these accounts. Is that because rolling over an old 401(k)-type account is hard to do? Not according to ING's Dan Greenshields, who estimated it takes about 15 minutes to roll over a retirement account into an IRA. It is more likely due to the lack of education provided by corporate fund managers and 401(k) custodians, who are insensitive to the current investment needs and risk-tolerance of retiring employees.

A word of caution about withdrawing a lump sum from your account: it is imprudent to do so unless you absolutely have to have the money. You will create an immediate and possibly severe tax event and will lose the future earning potential of the asset.

What about Risk Tolerance?

Risk tolerance is an individual thing. Some would never consider skydiving or bungee jumping and others will line up for the thrill. It's the same way with investing; different strokes for different folks. Two professors, Dr. Ruth Lytton at Virginia Tech, and Dr. John Grable at the University of Georgia, developed an Investment Risk Tolerance Quiz, a sampling of which follows. How would you answer:

1. In general, how would your best friend describe you as a risk taker?

○ A real gambler

○ Willing to take risks after completing adequate research

○ Cautious

○ A real risk avoider

2. You are on a TV game show and can choose one of the following. Which would you take?

○ $1,000 in cash

○ A 50% chance at winning $5,000

○ A 25% chance at winning $10,000

○ A 5% chance at winning $100,000

3. You have just finished saving for a "once-in-a-lifetime" vacation. Three weeks before you plan to leave, you lose your job. You would:

○ Cancel the vacation

○ Take a much more modest vacation

○ Go as scheduled, reasoning that you need the time to prepare for a job search

○ Extend your vacation, because this might be your last chance to go first-class

4. When you think of the word "risk" which of the following words comes to mind first?

○ Loss

○ Uncertainty

○ Opportunity

○ Thrill

Those questions are somewhat transparent. Some of the questions, however, cut to the chase and ask you about actual investment scenarios, such as these two:

5. In addition to whatever you own, you have been given $1,000. You are now asked to choose between:

   ○ A sure gain of $500

   ○ A 50% chance to gain $1,000 and a 50% chance to gain nothing

6. In addition to whatever you own, you have been given $2,000. You are now asked to choose between:

   ○ A sure loss of $500

   ○ A 50% chance to lose $1,000 and a 50% chance to lose nothing

Some questions test with scenarios to determine to what degree you would take a chance, in order to realize an uncertain gain that is unlikely to materialize. Take this one for example:

7. Your trusted friend and neighbor, an experienced geologist, is putting together a group of investors to fund an exploratory gold mining venture. The venture could pay back 50 to 100 times the investment if successful. If the mine is a bust, the entire investment is worthless. Your friend estimates the chance of success is only 20%. If you had the money, how much would you invest?

   ○ Nothing

   ○ One month's salary

   ○ Three month's salary

   ○ Six month's salary

Those are just seven out of the 20 questions posed by the Lytton/Grable quiz. Like most such quizzes, their accuracy is not 100%, but they are an indicator of an individual's comfort level with risk. When it comes to risk, experience is a great teacher. To illustrate the point, when we were younger we took more chances, didn't we? Perhaps we didn't know our limitations. With maturity comes wisdom and we are less inclined to risk life and limb. At least that holds true for most of us.

Some who were heavily invested in the NASDAQ during the 1990s would actually borrow money to invest in any company whose name ended in "dot com." They were heavily at risk and just didn't know it. Experience taught them, and taught them well, however, when the tech bubble burst, it left them broke and heavily in debt. Had they taken the Lytton/Grable quiz before that market crash, their answers would no doubt have been different than afterwards. Bravery in the face of danger is often foolish.

We know some individuals who don't trust any financial institution. Those who survived the Great Depression still are wary of banks. Can you blame them? As many as 4,000 banks failed during the one year of 1933 alone, taking $140 billion of depositors' money with them. Those dollars were worth six cents in today's money, too.

In 2007, The *Cleveland Plain Dealer* reported that an Ohio contractor by the name of Bob Kitts found $182,000 in Depression-era cash hidden inside the walls of a bathroom he was hired to remodel. The original owner of the home was a wealthy businessman who obviously would rather hide money in the walls, rather than put it in a bank.

So how do you view investment risk? Investing in the stock market nearly always includes at least the ***possibility*** of losing some of the original investment – *all* of it in some cases. Professional money managers are able to calculate what is called "standard deviation" and use historical returns in a specific area of investment to project whether an investment will be comparatively and relatively reliable. A high standard deviation indicates a higher degree of risk. A low standard deviation indicates a lower degree of risk. But in the end, it is still a projection and the safety is comparative and relative.

It is customary these days for large corporations to pay large sums of money for risk management studies so they can manage their risk. The findings of these studies allow them to develop what they call "risk management strategies." A large shipping corporation, for example, is able to use the data of the prevailing ocean weather patterns along the world's shipping lanes and merge that data with other information, such as the age of their equipment and maintenance records, to help them determine the risk associated with shipping goods by sea.

The same thing works with finance. But just as no one could have predicted the wrecking of the Italian cruise ship Costa Concordia in 2012, no one can predict when the next market crash will occur. If the events of 2008 have taught us anything, it is that risk evaluation is not a perfect science and there is no chart, graph, or set of data, that can predict the future. Just because a person handles your portfolio doesn't mean they have your back. It is ultimately your responsibility to know where you have your assets positioned, and how you feel about that exposure.

So again, how do you personally feel about risk? That is your risk tolerance and no one but you can measure it. Some people use what we call the "sleep at night" barometer to measure risk tolerance. It is simple. Can you sleep at night? Or do you toss and turn, worrying about your investments. Do you anxiously pace the floor, waiting for the market to open? Then, do you sit glued to the computer screen straining at the streaming ticker symbols as they tick up and down? If you can't get a good night's sleep, your risk needle is pegging in the danger area and you need to make an adjustment. If you can sleep soundly then you are probably okay.

"During the last market meltdown I slept like a baby," said one investor. "Up all night crying!"

CHAPTER ELEVEN

Four Choices Regarding Risk

"Money is an excellent slave and a horrible master." - P. T. Barnum

Essentially, there are four things you can do with risk:

1. Accept the risk - That's right; you can just accept it. From our observations of the world of wealth and people's behavior regarding it, that's what most people do. They just accept it, because they don't really think there is anything they can do about risk. It is just out there. If it bites them, it bites them.

While we understand how they came by that passive mode of thinking, we don't agree with it. Many investors have for decades been indoctrinated into a "buy-and-hold" strategy, or as we like to refer to it, a "buy-and-hope" strategy. Even though market conditions have changed over the years to the point that buy-and-hold rarely works, old investing habits and ideas, even though they are passé, are hard to dislodge. When people put their assets in investments that are *all correlated* to the stock market, whether in the S&P 500, the Dow, the NASDAQ, or any other exchange that reflects the value of the stock market, they are essentially accepting the full risk of the stock market. Just because their portfolio contains a mixture (large cap, small cap, bonds, international funds, etc.) it does not mean they are diversified. They are still fully at market risk and have no good hedge to protect themselves against it.

"But isn't that just part of investing?" they ask.

That's what some of those who are in the business of selling shares of stock would like for you to believe. One couple who lost a bundle when the stock market collapsed in 2008, related how their broker attempted to console them with a metaphor about the tides.

"You know when the tide goes out, all the boats go down," said the broker. "But then when the tide comes back in, all the boats rise again."

The wife explained that, while that illustration sounded nice, she wasn't buying any of it.

"This was no tide going out," she said. "This was the entire ocean backing away from the beach a few miles, leaving our boat stranded in the mud!"

Her counter-metaphor was more on target than she knew. There was a time when the market would recede and advance, somewhat like the tides. A dependable pattern, right? Not too risky. But now that the decade of the 1990s has ended, the behavior of the market has become far too volatile to trust with a buy-and-hold approach.

2. Reduce the risk - Explore alternative investments that are not correlated with the stock market and spread a portion of your assets into these. Take Real Estate Investment Trusts for example. They are viable investments, yet they are not market-based. REITS, like anything that can increase or decrease in value, comprise risk. But it is not *market* risk. When bonds fade and stocks rise, the market tends to regard REITs as if they were dividend-paying growth stocks. It's only when just about everything is tanking, as was the case in 2008, that REITs get hammered. We are not necessarily recommending REITS, we just want to make the point that there are alternative investments that are not market-based. The idea is to reduce risk by diversifying.

Equipment Leasing is also not a market-related investment. Again, we are not necessarily recommending Equipment Leasing programs, either. We just want to show there are ways of reducing market risk by diversification. If you are unfamiliar with the concept, Equipment Leasing Funds invest in a portfolio of business essential equipment, such as trucks (you didn't think Big Brown owned all those trucks, did you?), cranes, bulldozers, and other tangible assets that can be repossessed, resold, and reused. It is a wide field that includes such big ticket items as ships and barges, rail cars, and aviation equipment. These funds are not for everyone, but they *can* provide regular income, and tax advantages in some cases, and can serve as a partial inflation hedge.

Other alternatives to market investing can be some forms of life insurance and some kinds of annuities in which there is predictable growth and minimal risk. There is no one-size-fits all, here, and no decision should be made without obtaining all the facts. The point is, don't be like the lemmings who rush off the cliff as a single herd when it comes to risk. How can we say this gracefully? If risk is all you know, then you need education.

3. Transfer the risk - We all have different forms of insurance for the various perils from which we wish to protect ourselves. If the house burns down, you don't want to have to go to your bank and pull out your savings to rebuild. So, you have fire insurance, which transfers that risk to an insurance company. The same goes for your cars. You have risk because you drive and the roads are dangerous. What if you have an accident and damage your automobile? Worse yet, what if you injure someone? Again, you transfer that risk to an insurance company when you pay your premiums.

You can transfer investment risk as well, by transferring some of your assets to products that give you guarantees. Have you ever bought an appliance and when you went to pay for it, the clerk asked you if you wished to purchase an extended warranty? The warranty cost you something, didn't it? Did you weigh the pros and cons before you answered yes or no? Most people do. It's just another of life's little choices. If your investment comes with a guarantee, you will give up something in return for that guaranteed return. You will in some way, shape, or form, pay something for that added security. But it may be worth it. This is especially true if you are approaching retirement and your resources turn from renewable to non-renewable. Generally speaking, guarantees are more attractive than projections, to those who are in the "retirement red zone" (five years on either side).

4. Manage the risk - If you have ever been to an art museum, you probably noticed how large some of the paintings were. Some of them cover an entire wall. When you stand close to them it's difficult to see what the paintings are all about. You have to back up and get the big picture. To get an accurate picture of the stock market, you have to back up and look at it over time. You can see the patterns better, and that can help you manage risk.

At the time of this writing, we have been in what we call a "sideways" stock market for well over a decade. We believe that when this is the case, you must manage your risk very carefully. In the decades of the eighties and nineties, more specifically from 1982 to 2000, the stock market returned an average of approximately 17.6% per year. During that period, the people who, as they say, "got the biggest bang for their buck", were those with the "buy-and-hold" approach. They would buy a stock, a mutual fund for example, and hold on to it, confident of good returns. That works well when we are in a clearly defined bull market. But, in a sideways market – where the market declines for two or three years, goes up for three or four, goes down again for a couple of years, then back up for three or four years – when you stand back and look at the pattern, you are, after all that time, essentially back where you started.

> *"A very important consideration: what if what you thought to be true about your investment strategy turned out not to be true? When would you want to know about it, and more importantly, when would you want to take action?"*
>
> *–Jon Maxson*

A lot of activity and very little accomplishment - jogging in place.

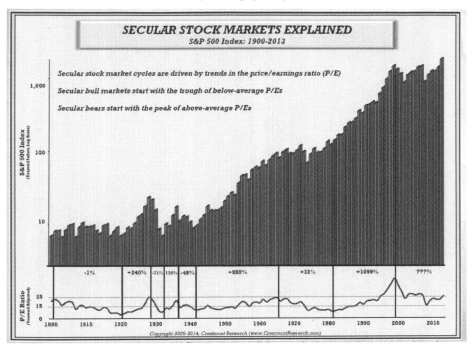

When we show this pattern to investors in our seminars, the tendency is to at first think, "Man, I'm in trouble. For 10 or 15 years I'm not going to make any money." The reason they think that way is because they don't know that they have other ***choices.*** You absolutely ***can*** make money in the stock market with a managed account. You employ retirement money managers to adjust your portfolio so that, when the market is going down, your investments do not go down as much. They adjust your investments so when the market goes down 40%, you may experience losses of 2% or 3% or 5% or 10% or 15%, but not necessarily 40%.

If you drop 40%, you need about 65% or so just to recover to the break-even point. But if you drop by a smaller number, you don't need nearly as much to get back to where you were. The reason most individual investors don't do this is because they don't have the time to manage their investments on a micro-level like professional money managers can. The philosophy we are advocating here is to employ a strategy that reduces risk, transfers risk, and manages risk, all at the same time. We believe merely accepting it, as if there were no other choices, is not a viable option.

CHAPTER TWELVE

Which Road Are You on with Your Financial Plan?

"In the house of the wise are stores of food and oil, but a foolish man devours all he has." - Proverbs 21:20

Putting together an objective analysis starts with listening. As we discussed in the previous two chapters, it is impossible to stamp out financial plans assembly line style, as if one size fits all. Financial plans are as individual as fingerprints – no two are exactly alike. To illustrate the point, you could take two adult males, same age, height and weight. Even make them identical twins if you wish. And let's even say they live across the street from each other, work at the same job, have the same size family, earn incomes identical to each other, and have the same net worth and savings. Their financial plans, however, would be different. Why? Because their goals are different and their values are not the same. How they view money and what they want it to do for them is not the same.

That is why, when we interview prospective clients at Beacon Capital Management, we start with nothing more than a notepad and a pen. We want to know what you think, feel, and expect, with regard to your finances and your financial future. Only then can we begin.

When we finally get to the part about an investment plan, we like to ask people which road they are on. They can be on one of three roads and, whether they know it or not, just about everyone that we meet in this process is on one of them.

The Walking Trail

The first road you can be on is what we call the investment walking trail. This trail is for a very conservative investor - very, very conservative. These are the investors who really can't stand any stock market risk at all in their portfolio. Look up the word "safety" in the dictionary and you would likely see their pictures beside it. Safety is their middle name. Returns? Sure they would like to have good returns, but they would give up the return factor in exchange for the assurance that their money is safe any day of the week.

To these individuals, walking into a bank gives them a good comfortable feeling, sort of the way a techie enjoys walking into a computer store, or a foodie enjoys the ambiance of a good restaurant. The atmosphere of the bank, with its marble floors, columns out front, and tellers behind counters, appeals to this person; it gives them a warm and fuzzy feeling. Now, you may chuckle at the idea of investing money with a bank, but what is this person thinking? Safety!

Banks are typically where most people park their immediate cash and short-term funds. We know the money is safe because we see the letters FDIC prominently displayed on the bank's wall and on the bank's stationery. The Federal Deposit Insurance Corporation, is an agency of the US Government charged with protecting consumers and keeping the banking industry as safe as possible. If the bank goes belly-up, the FDIC steps in so that bank customers don't lose all their money. This gives our walking trail investors great peace of mind.

Right now, on the walking trail, if all of your money is parked at the bank, you are probably getting a fraction of a percent in interest – usually a half percent. But even if you are fortunate enough to get 1% or even 2% you are still going backwards, because that doesn't even keep pace with inflation. What it boils down to is that you are accepting a different kind of risk – the risk of inflation gradually eroding your wealth. And like the erosion of a shoreline, it is imperceptible. You can't stand and watch it happen, but over time it becomes evident. Let's just say, for instance, that at 3% inflation, somebody has $50,000 in the bank, and they are using it as their current income source. In just 20 years, at 3% inflation, they will need $90,306 just to be able to buy the same goods and services. But what if inflation creeps up past the "manageable" 3% to 5%, which many people think is likely in the next two decades? That same $50,000 now needs to be $132,000. Jack up the inflation rate to 7% and your $50,000 would now need to be $193,484, or nearly four times the income of 20 years ago. Parking all your money on the investment walking trail may not be so safe after all.

The Interstate

Then, you have other people who are on the exact opposite end of the spectrum from the investment walking trail – they are on the investment interstate highway. This is where you put your money with a typical stock broker who just sells mutual funds, stocks and bonds. There are plenty of these out there. They utilize what we like to call "static management" strategies, otherwise known as buy-and-hold, buy-and-hope, or buy-and-pray. They are merely buying what they think are the best mutual funds or stocks at the time. Their mantra is that if it worked in the 1980s and 1990s it is bound to work today so they continue to employ the same strategies over and over.

Those on the investment interstate highway are working with brokers whose main job is to sell products. That's how they make their living. They are not planners with a fiduciary responsibility to their clients. Once they make their commissions, they are on to the next customer. Working with a typical broker, investors on the investment interstate can lose a considerable amount of money some periods and make very good money in other periods. In the years 2000, 2001, and 2002, for example, people lost as much as 50% to 60% of their portfolios using the buy-and-hold strategy recommended by their brokers. They were holding on as instructed, assured that if the market went down it would eventually come back. And of course, the market did come back, but it took a long time for these investors to get back to where they previously were. Then, there was another big wreck on the interstate. It happened all over again in 2008 and part of 2009, when the stock market lost another 50%.

S&P 500
January 3, 2000 – September 29, 2014

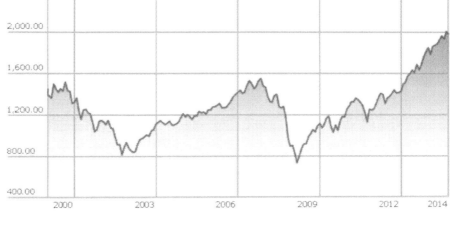

9/30/14, 2:33 PM   http://quotes.morningstar.com/indexquote/quote.html?ops=p&t=SPX&region=usa&cult

On the investment interstate you accept all the risk of the stock market. That's why we say you are at the other end of the spectrum from the walking trail investor. As we study history, there have been lots of different secular bear and bull markets and they recur periodically on a remarkably regular basis. In fact, if you study the stock market over the last 135 years, and look at the total return, minus inflation, you can clearly see on the chart that every bull market has been followed by a sideways market. The line on the graph goes up somewhat steadily, then there is a period of volatility where the line zigs and zags up and down, but essentially makes no progress. This goes on for a few years and then another bull market follows.

The first sideways market was from 1901 to 1921, lasting approximately 20 years. The second was from 1929 to 1948, a little over 18 years and the third lasted from 1963 to 1982. As this book is written, we are experiencing the current one which has been going on for some 14 years. The previous three sideways markets have averaged 19.3 years in duration, so a sideways market can last a relatively long time. People tend to forget that, because they focus on the 1980s and 1990s and how profitable those periods were for them in the stock market. That's why we say that using a buy-and-hold strategy in a volatile, sideways market, is a recipe for disappointment. What was it Einstein said about the definition of insanity? "Insanity is doing the same thing over and over again and expecting different results." If you are in the red zone of retirement, that is, within 5 - 10 years or closer, you are on the home stretch and it is crucial that you invest carefully. The interstate is a dangerous place for this age group.

The Investment Bike Path

So if you don't want to be on the walking trail where it is ultra-safe but you can't make a lot, and you don't want to be on the investment interstate, where a big crash could bring everything to a grinding halt, then where else is there? We recommend what we call the investment bike path. On the investment bike path you actually work with a true advisor. Registered Investment Advisors (RIAs) advise clients, they don't just sell products. They believe in a balanced approach of not having all your money in stocks, bonds, or mutual funds or in any one asset class. Registered Investment Advisors generally advocate asset class diversification where only some of your money is exposed to the market. Then, you utilize other investment options as well. Instead of selling products, as brokers and non-fiduciary advisors do, RIAs recommend a process that is carefully tailored to the investor's individual needs and risk tolerance.

To illustrate the difference between products and a process, think of the name of a great golfer. Tiger Woods perhaps. What do you think his golf clubs are worth? You can rest assured they are top of the line and cost a pretty penny. If you are a golfer, which would you rather have, Tiger's clubs or Tiger's swing? If you answered Tiger Woods' swing, you are absolutely right. That's not to say he doesn't require clubs to work his magic on the links; of course he does. But it's not the clubs that make him great; it's his swing. He needs a product. He needs a club. But his "secret," if you want to call it that, is in the swing.

You can get products anywhere. You can get them yourself. But what you really get from a Registered Investment Advisor with fiduciary responsibility is a process that will utilize all the financial tools available, to help you reduce, transfer, and manage risk, grow your portfolio; provide the income you need for the entire duration of your retirement. That is what the investment bike path is all about.

What Is a Fiduciary?

We have used the word fiduciary a few times. What is a fiduciary? The term, "fiduciary" comes from Latin word "fidere," which means "to trust." It has come to be a legal term that officially describes a relationship where an advisor is legally bound and contractually obligated to give a client advice that is in the client's best interest and not motivated by profit or remuneration. Fiduciaries are not allowed to be self-serving in their counsel. They may receive payment for their services, of course, but they are not to let that interfere with or influence their advice. They are not just after a commission, in other words. They are not salespersons. They are professional counselors who are legally obligated to tell you what is best for you, even if it fails to benefit them in any way.

CHAPTER THIRTEEN

Safety, Liquidity, High Returns – Pick any Two

"You make a living by what you get, you make a life by what you give" - Winston Churchill

When it comes to money, it's not how much you make that counts; it's how much you get to keep. When Benjamin Franklin coined the proverb, "A penny saved is a penny earned," he had no idea we would ever live in such a complex world, where wealth could be snatched away from us so easily. That's why we have given so much attention in this book to the measures we can take to preserve our wealth, once we have accumulated it. There are some tests we believe your money must pass if it is to be money enough for the rest of your life.

When you think about it, the three things people actually want from their investments are (a) safety, (b) liquidity, and (c) growth.

The perfect investment would be one where our principal is absolutely safe from risk, where we could access 100% of our money at any time, and we could receive guaranteed double-digit compounded returns. Unfortunately, such an investment doesn't exist.

A sign above a cash register in a small neighborhood store, whose livelihood was threatened by a nearby super store, read as follows:

Great Service, Quality Products, Low Prices – ***Pick Any Two!***

The three ingredients for a perfect investment may also come by way of compromise. For example, you may get capital preservation (safety) and liquidity, by giving up super-high returns in one investment. In another, you may be able to get great returns by taking on more risk. You get the idea.

If you have asset class diversification in your portfolio and your mixture of asset classes includes market investments as well as non-market investments, then what drops out the bottom is a fairly high degree of capital preservation, a high degree of liquidity, and the possibility of a high return – but it is not all in the same investment. As we said, there is no one investment that we know of where you can get all three.

Parking Places for Principal Protection

As discussed earlier, we all want good returns on our money, but it is difficult to get a good night's rest if we are in danger of losing our capital. So the objective, especially when we approach retirement, is to get as much safety, or capital preservation, as possible, without sacrificing too much in the way of liquidity and safety. We start by looking for principal-protected investments. How much of your principal needs to be safe from loss? Well, that depends on several things: your age, your risk tolerance, and your proximity to retirement. The younger you are, the more risk you can take on. The older you are, or the closer you are to retirement, the less risk you should take on.

Where can you put your money where your principal is guaranteed? What types of investments are available to you where you are guaranteed not to lose money? As we mentioned previously, you can put your money in a bank CD. Most people consider the FDIC a guarantee of safety, with good reason, but there are good times and bad times in any investment. Currently, this is a bad time to be involved in what people call "Certificates of Disappointment," since their rates of return are at an all-time low.

Another place you can go to is government bonds. You could look at treasuries and government bonds where your investment is backed by the full faith and credit of the United States government. If you believe the government has little chance of going out of business any time soon, then your money is safe there.

But what about the other two considerations: return and liquidity? You do have to tie up your money a very long time even to get 2% or 2.5% return, as this is written. We are not saying government bonds won't ever be a viable option for investment, but, in our estimation, you have to give up too much in the way of return and liquidity to get safety of principal.

Market Performance

No one has ever lost: Principal or Credited Interest **Fixed Index Annuity**

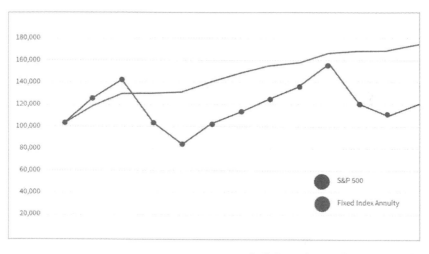

Past Performance is not an indication of future results

The third thing you can look into is an insurance product, something like a fixed annuity or a fixed indexed annuity. These are not FDIC insured, but they are principal-protected investments that can be linked to the growth of the stock market. These relatively new products track the movement of a stock market index. However, when the market is down, you are not negatively affected.

Fixed annuities are similar to CDs, but because they are insurance products and not bank accounts, they are not FDIC insured. However, they are solid investments, their underpinnings secured by both the state guaranty associations and the legal reserve. Like CDs, fixed annuities pay you a certain rate of return for a certain period of time. Currently, it is possible to lock in a five-year fixed annuity for around 3.25% a year, whereas a five-year CD may yield about half of that.

The kind of annuity we look to for both principal protection and a market-linked rate of return, is the fixed indexed annuity. With these instruments, whatever money you put in is protected from loss, even if the stock market goes down 30% or 40%. But if the market goes up, your account goes up subject to a cap. If the market goes up by, say, 15% you might get 7% or 8%. Once you do get your interest in that given year, it locks in at the end of the year and you can't ever lose that. This is called the ratchet-reset feature. Let's say you put $100,000 into a fixed indexed annuity and it goes up to $107,000 by the end of the year. If the stock market loses 20% the next year, the worst that could happen is your account stays at $107,000. Zero was your hero in that instance.

We do believe that with these products you can get a reasonable rate of return and still have principal protection. As far as liquidity is concerned, these instruments typically allow a withdrawal of 10% per year without penalty. Like CDs, you will pay a penalty for early withdrawal if you remove your money before the end of the surrender period, which is typically ten years.

Income Riders

One of the more attractive features to come along in recent years is the income rider. Since their introduction to fixed indexed annuities in the mid-2000s, they have become one of, if not the, most well-liked benefits ever developed by insurance companies. Voting with their pocketbooks, retirees and those approaching retirement did not seem to favor the old-style fixed annuities, where the only way to get a lifetime income was to annuitize, or surrender the account in exchange for the payout. The advent of the income rider has changed all that since it allows annuity owners to have a guaranteed lifetime income stream, and still pass on the unused portion of the annuity to their heirs at death.

Fixed indexed annuities with income riders attached have come to be known as "income annuities" or "hybrid annuities." According to the National Association for Fixed Annuities (NAFA), more than half of the people who buy fixed indexed annuities, choose to tack on the income rider.

How Do Income Riders Work?

There are a few moving parts to these annuities and the details vary from company to company, but let's start with this broad-brush explanation: Imagine a ledger sheet with two columns representing two accounts within the same annuity. One account is the **income account** and the other is the **accumulation account.** Insurance companies compete with brokerage houses, banks, and other insurance companies for your investment dollar, and many offer bonuses to attract customers. Let's say you deposit $500,000 and the company offers an 8% bonus. Both the income account and the accumulation account start out with a value that is $540,000.

The purpose of the income account is to serve as a base for calculating your lifetime income stream when you decide you want it. The longer you wait to "turn on" the income from the income account, the higher the value of this income account and the greater your income will be when activated.

Essentially, these two accounts run simultaneously, but the accumulation account grows according to a stock market index and the income account grows at a rate set by the insurance company. This will vary from company to company but is typically between **6%-8%.** That's the growth. When it comes to paying out, every insurance company has its own formula based on your attained age. A typical example, however, may be as follows: For easy math, let's say your income account has grown to $500,000. If you are between the ages of 70 and 74, and you decide to start your lifetime income, your annual payout will be calculated at 6%, or $30,000 per year. When you turn 75 you will be able to collect 6.5% of whatever is in the income account. Lifetime income payouts are deducted from the accumulation account. The unused portion of that account can be passed on to heirs.

While receiving these withdrawals, the annuitant is given two extremely precious guarantees.

1. Even though the yearly withdrawals are subtracted from the accumulation value, the extra interest carries on to be credited to the accumulation value, and the annuitant keeps access to the outstanding accumulation value at all times.
2. Even if yearly withdrawals eventually reduce the accumulation value, the carrier has to continue making the annual payments, so long as the annuitant lives.

Hybrid annuities are definitely not for everyone, but having at least a portion of your assets in them can help you reduce risk, and provide you with a guaranteed lifetime income. We believe they are something worthy of looking at if those two items are of

concern to you. We call it having **guardrails** on your finances.

Think of going across a long bridge suspended hundreds of feet above a deep mountain gorge. As you look down at the rushing rapids of a rock-strewn river far below, aren't you glad you have guardrails on either side of you? One such span is the Natchez Trace Parkway Bridge, located approximately 25 miles west of Franklin, Tennessee. Two giant concrete arches a quarter-mile long take cars over Star Route 96, and a heavily wooded valley 145 feet below. Even though the roadway is relatively wide as bridges go, it is difficult to imagine driving one car length across it without guardrails. Even the thought of it can make you shiver. Just as those guardrails represent security, safety, and protection for drivers, having money in principal-protected accounts can certainly be a great addition and complement to the portfolio of an investor who wishes to reduce risk.

CHAPTER FOURTEEN

Estate Planning Mistakes You Don't Want to Make

"When we are planning for posterity, we ought to remember that virtue is not hereditary" - Thomas Paine

When American businesswoman Leona Helmsley died in 2007, she left $12 million in a trust fund to her lapdog Trouble. Needless to say, her two disinherited grandsons weren't too pleased. The tiny Maltese, who was 12 at the time, lived out her last three years of life in luxury, blithely unaware how wealthy she was or how much the public hated her – or at least what she stood for. Helmsley was not called the "Queen of Mean" for nothing. Sadly, Trouble the dog passed away December 13, 2010, apparently from natural causes.

Talk about an estate mess! In 2008, a judge determined $12 million was too much to care for a fluffy, white dog and Trouble's inheritance was whittled to $2 million.

When Trouble died she left no will. According to a New York Times article dated June 9, 2011, the money left over in Trouble's trust went to charity.

Okay, so that is a bizarre case. But the truth is, many people create problems for the people they leave behind by either not planning properly or failing to plan at all. Death and dying are normally not the favorite topic of conversation around the dinner table, true. But they are an inevitable part of life. As the old Hank Williams song lyrics state, "I'll never get out of this world alive."

When faced with the idea of estate planning, some put it off because they think it is too costly, or too complex a process. That simply is not the case. Others respond with thoughts of "that's for rich folks" or "I'll let my children deal with all that when the time comes" or "I'll worry about that when I'm old," when in fact it is important for each and every person, young and old, and in any financial condition, to have a plan in place. The planning process does not have to be cold and detached; after all, it should be viewed as a celebration of life and accomplishments, and ensuring that future generations will benefit from your life's work.

Leona Helmsley isn't the only one who left behind an estate mess. Michael Jackson, the King of Pop, chose his aging mother to serve as the guardian for his children, with Diana Ross as a back-up, according to money.usnews.com. The article, which appeared December 6, 2001, said this created uncertainty about what would happen if his mother died before his youngest child became an adult. Would the children uproot their lives with family to live with Ross?

"Families turning their backs on each other and the value of the estate being diminished by legal fees—that is not just stuff that happens to celebrities," says estate lawyer Russell Fishkind in his book *Probate Wars of the Rich and Famous.*

Fishkind lists the following mistakes that celebrities make that we can take how-not-to-do-it lessons from:

1. Choosing inappropriate guardians - as in the case of Jackson. How long ago did you choose who would look after your children in the event of your demise? Is that relationship still the same? Are those individuals still willing and able to fulfill such a responsibility? Are your children grown and married with children of their own? Then that paragraph in your will is moot. Update your wills yearly.

2. Failing to update estate plans and account for complicated family situations - Anna Nicole Smith is probably the best (worst) example of this one. She was the *Playboy* centerfold who married billionaire oil tycoon J. Howard Marshall who later died. While she was fighting in court to claim his estate, her own will left everything to her teenaged son. Only problem, he died shortly before she did. To complicate matters further, she had a baby just before she died. The moral of the story is: update your wills regularly, especially after significant family events such as divorces, second marriages, and new children.

88

3. Having scattered financial accounts - How do you make sense out of an estate when there are myriad bank accounts, scattered investment accounts, and scattered documents, which is how Fishkind describes Jackson's estate? If your estate is that large, the least you can do is spend the money on an attorney to pull it all together for those you leave behind. Family members need to know where your important documents and assets are.

4. Appointing an executor with conflicts of interest - Grateful Dead guitarist Jerry Garcia, for example, named his third wife as executor of his estate, which led to conflicts between her and other family members after his death, Fishkind says. He adds that it is best to choose an unbiased person, such as a lawyer, to be the executor. (The executor does not need to be a financial or legal expert, but such expertise can certainly help.)

5. Paying too much in taxes - Sopranos star James Gandolfini, subjected his estate to unnecessary taxes. His will

> *"People need to make sure they know what their will says and consider whether they've explored powers of attorney, trusts and other vehicles for preserving and handing over wealth. Tax conditions and other factors require a plan that can adjust. It sounds simple, it's critical and still not done enough. You need to have a plan that is adaptive."*
> *–C. Pete Benson,*
> *Nashville Business Journal, August 10, 2012*

directed his executors to pay any estate taxes due before his assets were divided up among his heirs. Liz Weston, writing in an article entitled, "Five Celebrities Who Messed Up Their Wills", which appeared August 1, 2013, in MSN Money, said, "The problem is that any wealth left to his wife, Deborah Lin, could have avoided estate taxes entirely. (Although the federal estate tax can kick in on estates worth more than $5 million, you can leave an unlimited amount to a spouse without incurring a tax bill.)"

Fishkind says that Michael Jackson could have saved his estate millions in taxes by taking out a huge life insurance policy when he was a young man and putting it in trust. The idea is to anticipate estate taxes in advance, and strive to minimize them as much as possible through tools such as gifts to heirs, or trusts.

Health Care Powers of Attorney and Living Wills

Living Wills and advance directives regarding healthcare and end-of-life decisions, are documents that express the preferences and desires regarding medical treatments of persons who are later in a condition where they are unable to communicate their wishes, perhaps due to unconsciousness or terminal illness. They benefit those who want to avoid artificial life support as well as other more advanced medical procedures to sustain life, so they can have a natural death. The newspapers are full of unfortunate stories of individuals who are at the center of controversy because others have to determine what they think their wishes would have been. How much easier it would have been on all concerned if they had spelled them out. Many financial advisory firms these days have attorneys on their teams who specialize in providing these for clients. These documents also address the matter of organ donation, artificial resuscitation, and tube feeding. When these wills are valid, health care professionals respect them, and welcome them in carrying out the instructions of the individuals they represent.

The main reason why these wills are not put in place is because some surmise they are just for the sick and elderly. But these are important choices for anyone, since we could all end up dealing with accidents or sudden illnesses.

CHAPTER FIFTEEN

Choosing the Right Financial Advisor

"Wall Street is the only place that people ride to in a Rolls Royce to get advice from those who take the subway" - Warren Buffett

In his book *Confessions of a Happy Christian,* author and motivational speaker Zig Zigler tells the story of flying back to his home in Dallas. He notices the man sitting next to him is wearing his wedding ring on his index finger instead of the third finger on his left hand, which is what most people call the "ring finger."

Zig says he couldn't resist the temptation to comment on this anomaly, so he leans over and says, "Friend, I can't help but notice that you have your wedding ring on the wrong finger."

The man smiled and replied, "Yeah, I married the wrong woman!"

When undertaking any endeavor, whether it is business, personal, or financial, deciding whom you will partner with is crucial to the success of the venture. Choosing the right financial advisor can make the difference between having a happy, worry-free retirement, and one fraught with concern. The firm you select to assist you with your financial future needs to be a good match. The people you work with must have your interest at heart and share your values. The decision, of course, is a personal one, but there are several criteria it would be prudent to consider in making it. Here are a few:

Are they Independent?

What you don't want to do is select as your financial advisor someone who is an employee of a large firm. Whose interests do you think that individual will be representing – yours or the employer? Virtually anyone can hang out a shingle advertising himself or herself as a financial advisor. They may even be able to offer solutions to your financial problems, but at the end of the trail, the solutions will usually result in your buying products that the company is selling. It is not uncommon for such firms to have certain products or offerings that it is in their best interest to sell you. The managers tell their "advisors" what funds to recommend to clients, not because these funds are necessarily what you need to reach your investment goals, but because it benefits the brokerage house. The advisor's job is not necessarily to enhance your financial situation, but to increase the value of the company's stock shares and enhance the pocketbooks of shareholders. There is nothing illegal about this. Like any other enterprise in America, they are in business to make a profit. But if you choose a Wall Street brokerage firm as your advisor, you are unlikely to find individuals who will educate and inform you, and then allow you to make independent choices. An independent advisor has no obligations except to you. An independent financial advisor answers, not to a board of directors, but to you and you alone.

Are You Dealing with a Fiduciary?

If you recall, this word was defined earlier in the book at the end of the twelfth chapter. The word connotes *a legal or ethical relationship of trust between two or more parties.*

In the financial world, a fiduciary has pledged to work for the interests of his or her client and swears to put that client's interests ahead of his or her own. The advice fiduciaries give is always client-driven as opposed to profit-driven. The best type of fiduciary is a Registered Investment Advisory Firm (RIA). This simply means that financial professionals within this firm have made an official pledge to place their client's interests ahead of their own, without exception. If they break this pledge they risk losing their license and their livelihood. RIAs are audited every year by state and or federal government securities regulators to ensure this is happening.

Do They Understand You?

Have you ever noticed that when you visit the doctor's office for your annual physical exam the nurse hands you a clipboard with several forms to fill out? It may irritate you to have to fill them out again when you gave them the same information last year, but the forms are necessary. Your health situation may have changed in the last 12 months. The doctor will ask you several questions during the face-to-face portion of the exam, too. Why? Because a good physician will want to know everything about you, physically, before he treats you. A competent doctor would never prescribe medication for you without first having a complete understanding of your physical condition and knowing what medication you are taking.

A competent financial advisor will be one who takes the time to thoroughly understand your financial situation. He or she will spend time listening to you so as to ascertain not only what your financial goals are, but why do you have those goals. They should also formulate a well-designed and strategic plan to execute your wishes. You want to work with a financial advisor who has no product to push and no other agenda to follow except yours.

Do They Think Like You?

By this we don't mean that they must agree with you on personal issues, or share your taste in music and entertainment. Of course not! But when it comes to your money it is crucial that they share your values. If you are nearing or in retirement, your resources are precious to you because of what they represent – independence and quality of life. If you are not willing to treat those assets as if they were fodder for the gambling casinos in Las Vegas, then neither should your advisor. And yet we have heard horror stories where that appears to have been the case – planners who have been insensitive to the age of their clients and where they are along the financial timeline. If you are like most families who are in the red zone of retirement, you have a path in mind. You need an advisor who will accompany you and help you over the obstacles in that path – not one who will attempt to lead you to a different path just because it is one more familiar to them. Let us give you an example:

In our RIA firm, our desire is to build strategies with the goal of reliable income for life without depleting all of your principal. When potential clients come to our office for consultations, the first thing we do is chat. We want to know what is on their minds. What are their notions about money and finances? We want to be able to match our thinking with theirs so we can work together. But if we can't, there is no need to proceed. We part as friends, but we know we are not a match for everyone and we do not try to be.

Sometimes we find it useful to ask potential clients to pretend that all their money was cash and stacked up in their living room. Sounds crazy, but it helps put things in perspective. Here's all this money; what should you do with it? You can't just leave it there. If you invest it, what should be the primary attribute of this investment? What do you want the money to do for you and your family? We usually find that after this kind of a conversation, we and our clients share the same core beliefs about money and the path forward becomes easier to chart. Our priorities are usually in the same order:

1. Principal Protected Strategies.
2. Growth/Income/Returns.
3. Taxes/Fees.
4. Liquidity.

Yes, principal protection first of all, then growth. Keep in mind that we specialize in handling cases where the individual is approaching or in retirement. Our philosophy at Beacon Capital Management is, it's not the money you make but the amount you get to keep that counts. What good is growing your wealth only to let it slip away?

How Are They Compensated?

In your search for the right advisor, be sure to find out how the advisor candidate is paid. If *you* are paying them, then they work for you. If a brokerage house, or some other major firm, is paying them, then they *don't* work for you, they work for someone else. It's as simple as that. Don't be embarrassed to ask, "How are you compensated?" That is not a personal question; it is a business question. It is appropriate fact-finding. You are not asking to be nosy or to find out the advisor's yearly salary or net worth. You want to know if there are possible conflicts of interest or hidden fees and charges. Knowing how your advisor is compensated may help you understand and evaluate how objective he or she will be in any recommendations you receive. True professionals will not mind this dialogue between client/advisor at all.

How Will They Work With You?

There should be a high level of communication between you and your financial advisor. Do not hesitate to ask what the firm's policy is on periodic reviews of your portfolio. Also, ask who will be handling your account. Will it be farmed out to a third-party firm, or given to a rookie associate to manage? Or will the advisor candidate you are interviewing be the one who personally handles the account. If other team members will be involved in managing your account, wouldn't it be a good idea to meet and get to know them?

When you call the number of the office, will a human answer the phone during business hours? Or will you have to listen to a series of impersonal prompts that ask you to enter information repeatedly, only to be connected to someone's voice mail? We know some people are computer literate and up to date on modern technology. They understand voice mail when the person they are calling is unavailable. But they get frustrated when they have to press one for English and two for Spanish, then digitally enter their date of birth, pin number, account number, and zip code, only to have to listen to another menu of choices. We can't say we disagree with them.

How Much Experience Do They Have?

If you are like most people, you don't relish the idea of being a guinea pig. Ask about experience. How long has the candidate for your business been advising clients? How did their clients fare in the last market crash? How successful has your advisor candidate been at providing solutions that ensure guaranteed income for his or her clients in retirement. Ask what services the firm offers. Are they able to offer a well-rounded approach, or is their focus so narrow that they only know one path? Remember Maslow's concept, "If the only tool you have is a hammer, you tend to see every problem as a nail." Are they holistic in their approach to financial planning?

Holistic medical treatment involves treating the "whole" person. Likewise, holistic financial planning shuns the one-size-fits-all approach. It is comprehensive planning that looks beyond rate of return and addresses the end goals of the client. Some call it "life planning", with an emphasis on the financial. More and more people want to make sure their money will do what they want it to do. Holistic planning involves every aspect of your financial life. It is based on the idea that your money should have a purpose; otherwise, it is merely numbers on paper.

Some people come into the offices of Beacon Capital Management and know exactly what they want to do with their wealth. With those clients we become facilitators. We help them execute their plans. Other folks don't really know what they want. With them our work is that of educators. We help them visualize the future, and translate the possible application of their resources to their individual personal circumstances. If it sounds corny to talk in terms of people's deepest needs, goals, desires, and dreams, we don't apologize. As "touchy-feely" as that sounds, when it's your life, it takes on a different feel altogether.

Holistic planning takes a multi-disciplinary approach to financial planning, and involves developing a team of professionals who can deliver investment, retirement, and estate planning. All advisor teams should include a financial planner, a CPA, and an Estate Planning Attorney. Key players, in addition to those, could include a Business Attorney, Insurance Agent, Business Broker, etc. However, coordinating such a team can be daunting and intimidating for the client, so the Holistic Planner acts as the liaison between the client and the advisor team.

What other services do they offer?

Service is important in financial planning. How often will they meet with you to discuss your progress? The financial landscape is constantly changing; your needs and thinking may change, too. You need to meet with your advisory firm at least once a year, maybe more often, to keep pace with these changes.

Lastly, do you like this person? What is your gut telling you about him or her? Don't ignore this. Your gut instinct is mostly right in measuring trust. Feelings, after all, are facts. Do you feel that you can trust this individual to be an advocate for you in this important area of life?

Retail Versus Institutional Investing

As everyone knows, it's better for the old wallet if you can buy it wholesale. When it comes to investing, large corporations and institutions are at an advantage when it comes to pricing and selection. There is no reason why smaller investors cannot enjoy that same advantage. It all depends on the financial advisor you choose.

There is a tremendous advantage when ordinary folks have the services of institutional-level advisors and consultants. These professionals can often help investors bypass the additional costs of the retail brokerage market. Institutional account holders generally trade directly, without the extra costs associated with retail distribution and marketing. Call it cutting out the middle man if you wish, and, in the bargain, getting someone who will tell you the truth, the whole truth, and nothing but the truth, about your financial affairs. Individual investors who receive institutional-level advice benefit from having professional managers and financial planners focusing on their overall allocation, and the active movement of capital to attractive areas from unattractive ones. It's the difference between active management and the staid "buy-and-hold" philosophy of investing that is no longer an effective way to navigate the risks presented by today's geographically diverse, fast-paced financial markets. This is especially true for retirees. Of all investor classes, these folks are making critical allocation decisions with the portion of their portfolios they place in the stock market. They deserve full-time, institutional-level professionals working on their behalf and directly accountable when making the really important investment allocation decisions.

It's Worth the Effort

Selecting the right retirement advisor will require some work on your part, but it's worth it when you consider just how critical your decisions about money are as you approach retirement. Getting it right is the difference between losing sleep and having peace of mind. Selecting the right guide for this part of your financial journey can mean being able enjoy your Golden Years, instead of worrying about them. Let's face it – retirement is unfamiliar territory. There is the possibility for great adventure, but also potential danger if you fail to prepare properly. To make sure you take the right steps, you want as a guide an individual who knows the landscape and can get you through it safely, with money enough for the rest of your life.

Acknowledgements

Over the many years we have been counseling families about their financial goals and plans, we have heard time and time again, "I just hope we have enough money to get us through the rest of our life." This major concern and challenge facing people today is what inspired us to write *Money Enough for Life?* Our hope and prayer is that as people learn and implement the principles of this book it will give them renewed confidence that they will not run out of money before they run out of life. With pensions going away and people living longer there is growing anxiety among investors concerning their current financial planning and needs. Our goal is to provide information through the pages of this book that will be an antidote to those fears and concerns.

For those of you who are reading our book, we applaud you for taking the time to become educated on financial matters. Society as a whole seems to offer very little in the way of sound, practical financial advice, and the education system puts little or no effort into helping students learn about budgeting, keeping out of debt and investing for their future. The onus is upon us to educate ourselves and pass it on to those we care about, which we hope you will continue to do.

There are so many people to thank for helping us complete this project. No one deserves praise and credit more than our spouses – Jon's wife, MaryAnn and Pete's wife, Ginnie – who have been incredibly helpful, supportive, and our biggest cheerleaders. Their support for our business and the sacrifices they make so that we can give our best to our clients is nothing short of amazing. We just can't thank you enough. In addition to our wives, we have felt tremendous support from other immediate family members as well.

This book would not have been possible without the tremendous support from our dedicated staff. We are truly blessed to be surrounded by such hardworking and efficient individuals.

You would not be holding this book were it not for our copy editor Tom Bowen. His encouragement and expertise guided us and motivated us to finish this project when it would have been tempting to just give it up. Also we want to give a shout out to Pat Brown, Pete's sister in law, who also contributed greatly in the tedious editing work. In addition, we would be remiss not to commend and thank Mallory McDaniel and Annie Branson and the entire creative department at Advisors Excel for their invaluable assistance in getting this information into printed form.

Last, but certainly not least, we want to thank our Lord and Savior Jesus Christ! He deserves glory and praise for His goodness and for the many blessings He brings to our lives each and every day. We owe our very lives and futures to Him!!

"Now to Him who is able to do immeasurably more than all we ask or imagine, according to his power that is at work within us, **to Him be glory** in the church and in Christ Jesus throughout all generations, for ever and ever! Amen." Ephesians 3:20.

About the Authors

Pete Benson

Pete Benson grew up on Grand Manan Island, New Brunswick, Canada, an island of quaint fishing villages about as far removed from the hubbub of urban life as you can get. If you have ever heard of the Bay of Fundy, a place famous for extreme high and low tides, then you know where Pete called home in his youth. Grand Manan sits at the mouth of that large body of water where the tides can fluctuate as much as 20 feet.

Fishing, in one form or another, is the backbone of the island's economy, followed by tourism in the summer, especially after Reader's Digest listed Grand Manan as one of the top 10 islands in the world to visit. Pete's father was a lobster fisherman and his grandfather owned a herring processing plant where Pete worked growing up.

Grand Manan is a 90-minute ferry ride from the Canadian mainland. Ironically, Pete's boyhood home is situated geographically closer to the United States than Canada. If the ferry could go back and forth to the state of Maine the ride would take half the time. Life was self-sustaining, for the most part, on the 21-by-11-mile island, but trips to Saint John on the mainland were necessary for shopping, dentist and doctor appointments, and the like.

Pete's Dad and both of his grandfathers were hard-working entrepreneurs who believed a little hard work never hurt anyone. Pete describes them as men of deep faith with strong conservative values of thrift and generosity of spirit. "They instilled in me the attitude that faith in God was something to be proud of and vocal about," Pete says. "They also helped me believe I could become or accomplish anything I really applied myself to."

Pete learned early on that the life of a fisherman was not for him. On his first serious outing with his father he discovered he was chronically prone to seasickness.

Pete is literally married to "the girl next door," Ginnie, who was his high school sweetheart. They grew up seven houses apart. Ginnie's and Pete's parents were friends, and the two families attended the same small church in the same small village. They have been married 38 years and are parents to three children, Ginger, Amanda, and Daniel, and have seven grandchildren. Pete and Ginnie are dual citizens of both the United States and Canada. They raised their family in Canada for the early years and then moved South in 1989. Pete and Ginnie live in Franklin, Tennessee, a rapidly growing suburb of Nashville. A few years ago they built a summer home on Grand Manan and make it back to visit several times a year.

Pete graduated from high school in 1977 and entered Kingswood University in Sussex, New Brunswick. Always the "people person," Pete wanted to make a difference, and found fulfillment in helping others when he entered the ministry. Pete's entire family was deeply religious and by his own account, Pete was like a sponge growing up. He learned industry, thrift, and the value of a relationship with God, from his parents and grandparents on both sides. His father, James W. Benson, passed away in 2008, and his mother, Frances E. Benson, age 80, lives in a nursing home at the time of this writing. He credits his family members with giving him a spiritual heritage that he treasures to this day. Pete obtained his Master's degree in Counseling from Eastern Nazarene College in Boston, Massachusetts in 1988.

In the mid 90's Pete discovered a passion for helping people with their finances and began developing his education in that direction. This grew into a vision of owning a business that focused solely on providing honest, simple, and customized financial advice, for people of all ages. That vision has since expanded and given Pete opportunities to speak to groups, churches, and at conferences in the U.S., Canada, and Europe. Pete now serves on the board of his alma mater, Kingswood University; the Board of Southern Wesleyan University; as well as the board for Platinum Advisors in central Florida and also serves on the advisory board for the Buckingham Leadership Institute in Sussex, N.B., Canada. He and Ginnie are both volunteers in their home church in Nashville and also support other non-profit organizations around the globe.

Pete is a founding co-owner of Beacon Capital Management with his business partner, Jon Maxson. Together they have built a successful, full-service firm that is well-recognized in the Middle Tennessee area. Pete loves solving problems and being in what he calls a "people business."

"We want families to have a well thought out **strategic plan** for their financial future…not just a hope," Pete says. "Our focus is *total* wealth management, not just money accumulation." One of Pete's favorite maxims is "Make a little money first and make a little money last."

Pete refers to the financial plans he builds for his clients as "roadmaps for retirement", with primary emphasis on income planning. He believes that people need true asset-class diversification with their market-based investments. The mission of Beacon Capital Management is to first educate clients, then identify problems and finally, find solutions!

Jon Maxson

Some people like to lay claim to rural roots by saying they grew up on a farm, but Jon Maxson really did. His paternal grandfather, Clair

Maxson, owned a 120-acre dairy farm in very rural West Edmeston, New York, and as early as Jon can remember, he was feeding livestock, putting up hay, milking cows, mending fences, and performing just about any other task that would qualify as farming.

Like many who had to face the economic reality of life on a family farm, his father, Robert Maxson, farmed, and worked a second job as a machinist for the Proctor and Gamble plant in nearby Norwich, New York, for 43 years before he retired. Jon says that any job is light work after putting up 3,000 bales of hay.

One of the carryovers from farm work is Jon's habit of rising at 4 a.m. while it is dark outside and the rest of the world is asleep. "It's an old habit," he says. "I read, and go to the gym and work out. To say I am a morning person would be putting it mildly."

Jon says the life lessons he learned from his parents and grandparents benefit him to this day. He tells the story of how his parents taught him the value of money when he was 12. His parents had given him a monthly allowance. The money burned a hole in Jon's pocket and he spent it foolishly as soon as he had the first opportunity. His parents tried an experiment. They gave Jon 100 egg-laying, full-grown chickens, and enough grain to feed them for a month. They even helped him build a small out-building in which to house the birds and equipped the coop with all the paraphernalia that goes with chicken farming. Jon's chicken business boomed. He collected the eggs each morning and washed them, placed them in cartons, and sold them. Jon admits he didn't grasp his lesson in economics until he ran out of feed and, having spent his profits, had only $8.00 to invest in more.

"The lesson I learned from that is, if you are involved in any enterprise where there is profit and expense, feed the business first," Jon says.

Long summers spent helping his grandfather work in the fields were formative. His grandfather had lived through the Great Depression and suffered from Polio as a child, leaving him with one useful arm.

"It was amazing what that man could do with one good arm," Jon states. "He loved iced tea and used to mount a big cooler of it on the back of the hay baler during summertime. At break time he would share with me some of the principles of living a good life. He talked with me a lot about character and integrity.

"He didn't lecture me," Jon says. "He just sat there on the back of that hay baler and drank iced tea, and told me stories and taught me principles that echoed in my head for years. To this day I can't drink a glass of iced tea without remembering some of the things he taught me. He died in 2012, at age 93."

Jon left home at age 17 after he graduated high school, to work his way through Tennessee Temple University. He received his Bachelor's Degree in Psychology and Business after four years, during which time he worked at sandwich shops, hotels, delivered papers, washed windows, and went back home in the summers to bale hay. He met his wife, Mary Ann, during the second week of his freshman year.

"I was washing the windows of the university library when I saw her walking by," he says of Mary Ann. "I just thought she was amazing." They married in 1992.

At 21 years of age, Jon tried his hand at several career opportunities before landing a job with AT&T, and he began climbing the corporate ladder at a rapid pace. Along the way he furthered his education by taking courses in finance at University of Tennessee at Chattanooga, and soon became a market manager with AT&T.

After nine and a half years with AT&T, Jon came across an opportunity to put his training in finance to work and decided to make a change. It would require him leaving a promising career in corporate America, but the timing seemed right for him to go in a different direction when Ginnie Benson, a director at AT&T, introduced Jon to Pete. The two men began conversations that would ultimately lead to a business partnership and the start of Beacon Capital Management.

"A lot of things just seemed to be moving us in that direction," explains Jon of the way he and Pete began their partnership which, as this is written, is going on its second decade. "Pete was looking for a business partner who shared his personal business philosophy and I wanted to do something that would have a more direct impact on people's lives."

Jon describes his mother and father and his grandparents on both sides as people "deeply rooted in their faith."

"I have several relatives who are involved in the ministry and a strong belief system that runs in the family," he says.

Jon and Mary Ann live in Franklin, Tennessee, and have been married for 22 years. They are the parents of three boys, Nathan, Noah, and Nealan. Jon enjoys playing soccer with his boys and attending UT football games. Additionally, he loves to take his boys fishing at local ponds and streams and go camping with them. He says being a good dad is just passing on what he was given growing up.

"I am trying to pass a family tradition of integrity to my boys," he declares. They have a maxim they have memorized and have even taped to their mirrors. It reads as follows:

A man of Integrity:

- Loves Jesus
- Tells the truth
- Does what is right
- Works hard and finishes the job
- Loves his family and others
- Takes care of Mom

39324243R00070

Made in the USA
Charleston, SC
04 March 2015